Palgrave Studies in Globalization and Embodiment

Series Editors

Erynn Masi de Casanova
University of Cincinnati,
Cincinnati, Ohio, USA

Afshan Jafar
Connecticut College,
New London, Connecticut, USA

This cutting-edge series will address how global forces impact human bodies and the individual and collective practices associated with them. Books in this series will explore the globalization of bodily practices as well as how the interaction of local and global ideas about bodies produces particular forms of embodiment. We are particularly interested in research covering the ways that globalization engenders inbetween spaces, hybrid identities and "body projects."

More information about this series at
http://www.springer.com/series/15115

Loh Han Loong Lionel

The Body and Senses in Martial Culture

Loh Han Loong Lionel
Singapore

Palgrave Studies in Globalization and Embodiment
ISBN 978-1-137-55741-4   ISBN 978-1-137-55742-1   (eBook)
DOI 10.1057/978-1-137-55742-1

Library of Congress Control Number: 2016938232

Printed on acid-free paper

This Palgrave Pivot imprint is published by Springer Nature
The registered company is Nature America Inc. New York

CONTENTS

CHAPTER 1

Introduction

Abstract As a case study of somatic cultures, this ethnographic study of a mixed martial arts (MMA) gym in Thailand examines the processes by which individuals come to embody particular bodily techniques and values. Of interest is the interrelationship between cultural understandings of bodily knowledge and the way individuals utilise their bodies. This chapter provides a conceptual understanding of this ethnographic study by examining the eclectic body of literature dealing with martial arts and the body, phenomenology and the senses, and sporting bodies and masculinities.

In *Techniques of the Body*, Mauss (2006) examines how culture mediates the way individuals come to think about the world vis-à-vis bodily knowledge and the way they utilise their bodies. As a case study of somatic cultures, this ethnographic study of a mixed martial arts (MMA) gym in Thailand examines the processes by which individuals come to embody particular bodily techniques and values. Since martial arts are often perceived to be an inherently masculine activity, maintaining and performing their identity as masculine fighters is often central to the men's journey of embodying martial disciplines. Issues of masculinity and embodiment are closely intertwined in this ethnographic study and I detail how cultural norms and values are perpetuated and sustained through the gym's daily regimes and the informal sanctions applied against those who fail to conform.

Given how this field site caters mainly to foreign men, I then decon-struct the men's willingness to embark on a sojourn in Thailand in order to indoctrinate their body within a particular martial tradition. Martial arts can be said to be foreign to all bodies because in today's contempo-rary milieu, martial arts is often not part of the everyday, few individuals are socialised into martial disciplines and acts of violence are not nor-malised. This is further exacerbated in the context of foreigners travelling to Thailand to learn Muay Thai, a martial art that is coloured with spe-cific cultural and nationalistic overtones (Junlakan and Prayukvong 2001; Loh 2011; Toh 2002; Vail 1998). Transnational flows not only impact the discursive construction of martial arts and I will later illustrate how these transnational flows also facilitate the men's quests and motivations to learn martial disciplines. Muay Thai has been gaining presence on the global stage (Bangkok Post 2008; Bohwongprasert 2003; Norjidi 2009; Thai News Service 2011; Yip 2011). The recently concluded 11th World Wai Kru Muay Thai Ceremony on 12 March 2015, which saw numer-ous competitors and Thai boxing enthusiasts from diverse countries such as the UK and Ukraine congregating in Thailand, reflects the increasing popularity of Muay Thai globally.

Through the lived realities and everyday experiences of these fight-ers, I seek to examine (1) why foreigners invest their time and money to train in martial arts in Thailand, (2) the linkages between the embodi-ment of martial arts and masculinity, (3) how foreign bodies consume martial arts and what they get out of it, (4) the sensory reconfiguration required of a fighter, and (5) the impact of transnational flows on bodily dispositions and knowledge. This phenomenon of transforming the body can be situated within a period of ontological anxiety where individu-als, "becom[ing] responsible for the design of [their] bodies" (Giddens 1991, 102), engage in self-reflexive projects concerning their bodies and social selves. For Giddens, this anxiety arises from individuals being able to shape their own bodies, challenging preconceived boundaries of what the body can be. This implies a personal responsibility for the shape one is in, yet there is no fixed idea of the ideal form that should be attained. The men at the gym are expected to discipline their bodies, and failure to do so often results in sanctions. Featherstone's (2007) concept of body projects is often used to explain a wide array of activities ranging from bodybuilding to cosmetic surgery (cf. Atkinson 2008; Brown and Graham 2008; Crossley 2006). For Featherstone, bodies are projects that require constant disciplining and work because the body is the symbolic edifice upon which identity formation occurs. Individuals engage in these body projects to create a sense of identity and find solidarity within particular somatic cultures. Similarly, within the literature on sports, the body, subjected to scientific discourses, becomes a relentless project for perfection and excellence (Bryson 1990; Konig 1995; Tuxill and Wigmore 1991; Voy 1991). A critique of conceptualising the body as a project is that it assumes that individuals embody rationality and fails to consider how the body is subjected to physiological limitations and affective dimensions (Shilling 2008). Through my informants' narratives, I portray the tensions experienced by these men as they oscillate between scientific discourses, societal norms, and the limitations of the body.

In the subsequent section, I will outline the bodies of literature that provide theoretical insights into this localised phenomenon that has global linkages. The phenomenological tradition, reiterating the importance of the body and senses in somatic cultures, unifies the literature pertaining to masculinity and martial arts. Next, I will provide brief summaries of the subsequent chapters, sketching my theoretical arguments and its relationship to my research problematic.

MARTIAL ARTS AND THE BODY

Tan (2008) succinctly summarises and charts the gradual development of academic interest in martial arts over the last few decades. He charts a chronological break between the period up to the 1990s and that from the 1990s to the present. He charges that in the former period, a majority of studies tended to "possess a fairly ahistorical, quantitative, positivistic and clinically-driven analysis of martial arts" (2008, 69) that failed to contextualise martial arts or pugilism as a microcosm that reflects different socio-cultural contexts, symbolism, and meanings that constitute the lived experiences of practitioners. The latter period, in which there is more qualitative and in-depth theorising of martial arts, is one in which numerous theorists have attempted to conceptualise and problematise martial arts in relation to anthropological and sociological enquiries, and have linked martial arts to other issues such as nationalism, politics, power, popular culture, ritual studies, and the body. Some keystone works include Donohue's (1991) ethnographic study, *The Forge of the Spirit: Structure, Motion, and Meaning in the Japanese Martial Tradition*, in which a structural-functionalist approach was utilised to analyse Aikido, Judo, and Kendo. Donohue was interested here in how the ritual practices of these martial arts are metonymic of larger social and cultural values/norms. In another study, *Warrior Dreams: The Martial Arts and the American Imagination*, Donohue (1994a, b) highlights the myriad reasons why individuals consume martial arts. Some see it as a system of self-defence; others are drawn by its connections to popular culture or fantasy. This consumption, he argues, is linked to the "essentially emotional and aesthetic pull" (2002, 66) exerted by martial arts on individuals. For Donohue (1991, 1994a, b, 2002), the interest in foreign martial traditions stems not only from the sense of solidarity that martial arts creates amongst its practitioners but also because they can serve as a ritualistic performance that functions as a "shield against [the existential] terror [of uncertainty]" (Berger 1967, 22). These rituals give shape/framework to everyday life, providing individuals with discipline, mental fortitude, and opportunity to know themselves better.

The authors in Jones (2002) also took up this thread of exploring the performativity of martial arts. In terms of geographical coverage, until recently, more attention was paid to Japanese martial arts. Recent studies of non-Japanese martial arts include Indian martial arts (Alter 2002; Zarrilli 1998), Chinese martial arts (Alexander 2009; Holcombe 2002; Shahar 2008), boxing (Glogower 2009; Wacquant 1995, 1998, 2004, 2005), MMA (Van Bottenburg and Heilbron 2006; Downey 2007; Garcia, and Malcom 2010; Spencer 2009), Pencak Silat (Farrer 2009; Lee 2009), Capoeira (Delamont and Stephens 2006, 2008), and Muay Thai (Nur Amali 2001; Pattana 2005, 2007; Satterlund 2006; Toh 2002). Focusing on the effects of globalisation, the authors in Green and Svinth (2003) have also analysed some of the processes of modification and change that different martial arts have undergone.

Despite the increased attention being paid to martial arts, it must be recognised that there still remains a lacuna regarding martial arts within the sociology of sports (Van Bottenburg and Heilbron 2006; Garcia and Malcom 2010). Studies on martial arts seldom take them as the focal point of analysis but rather utilise them as a lens through which one can comprehend motifs of power, gender, structure, and agency. In addition, the martial arts are often analysed in a discursive manner by researchers who are not themselves practitioners. By discursive, I am referring to how most sociological analysis of the martial arts is the product of Foucauldian discourses or is being textually mediated by linking them to other discourses. For example, Ashkenazi (2002) examines how through discourses, Karate, a Japanese martial art, is constructed as a microcosm of the ideal Japanese society, intimately intertwined with evaluations and conceptions of the existing social order. Individuals join the Karate community because it furnishes them with the necessary social and cultural capital that will stand them in good stead in their working life. Membership in a university Karate club not only signifies that the individual has internalised laudable social values such as mental and physical fortitude but also provides him with a network of contacts in the working world. In short, "Karate practices, like rituals, are homologous to circumstances some people want to perceive in their society: a reflection of presumed order" (2002, 110). Any concern with the visceral sensations of bodies in martial arts is often subsumed by concerns about how bodies are disciplined by discourses. In academic works on martial arts, studies of embodied experiences, taking a phenomenological approach, are few compared to studies of performance, about creating an impression on an audience, or studies drawing upon discourse analysis. Another example would be Shahar's (2008) discussion of how the corporeality of Shaolin monks is impacted by prevailing discourses that structure and discipline their bodies within a particular socio-cultural milieu. Shahar's detailed analysis of the disciplining of bodies through the top-down imposition of power again neglects the corporeal aspect. This discursive treatment of martial arts, as opposed to a paradigm that explores how the intersubjective practices constitute the embodied intentionality behind an action (Gibson 1979, 218–219), is reflective of different ontological and epistemological assumptions about the world. Discursive constructions of martial arts often implicitly rest upon Platonic–Cartesian conceptualisations of the self. This Cartesian dualism of mind and body views the mind as the seat of rationality, language, thought, and knowledge, diametrically opposed to the body as the source of banal irrationality and emotions (Farnell 1999; Shilling 2007; Turner 1984; Van Wolputte 2004). Farnell (1999, 346) succinctly summarises how this bifurcation has valorised the written and spoken signs as being:

> …'real' knowledge, internal to the reasoning mind of a solipsistic individual, to the exclusion of other semiotic (i.e. meaning-making) practices, thereby bifurcating intelligent activities. This, in turn, has produced a radical disjunction between verbal and so-called nonverbal aspects of communication in our meta-linguistic discourse.

In response to this disembodied treatment of social phenomena, which ignores the intentionality and intersubjectivity of action, social theorists have sought to reconceptualise issues of embodiment. They have shifted away from perceiving the body as a cultural construct, to talking phenomenologically about and from the body as a source of action (see Crossley 1995, 1996, 2007; Frank 1991; Hockey and Allen-Collinson 2009; Howson and Inglis 2001; Shilling 1993, 2008; Turner 1984). In the study of somatic cultures such as dance and martial arts, where the corporeality of the body, as the medium and repository of experiential knowledge (Mellor and Shilling 1997), is often brought to the forefront of social interaction, being a practitioner, I argue for the need to develop a more comprehensive knowledge about martial arts that is not simply textually mediated. Rather than subscribe to a dichotomy that views the body as either a subject or an object, the constant oscillation of the body as both subject and object needs to be addressed (see Loh 2010). To address this gap in the literature, there is then a need to perceive martial arts through the lens of the lived body, the agentic body of meaning-giving (Honkasalo 1998, 41) vis-à-vis the physical and social milieu. This is the theoretical impetus behind this ethnographic study of Muay Thai.

Phenomenology, the Body and the Senses

The mind–body dualism that still prevails in the literature on martial arts may be attributed to the continuing dominance of a Husserlian paradigm in phenomenological schools of thought (Moustakas 1994; Schutz 1967). Husserl (1960[1931]) asserts that all conscious acts are derived from the mind and that sensory feedback from the body is processed first by the mind before the individual acts. This has led to a lacuna in establishing a methodology that resonates with phenomenology's ontological and epistemological status (cf. Katz and Csordas 2003). In addition, the Husserlian paradigm further perpetuates ocularcentrism and Cartesianism (Spencer 2012). Descartes's (1998[1641]) mind–body dualism, which posits the superiority of the "rational" mind over the "irrational" and "unruly" body, is a spectre that still haunts paradigms in social research (Burkitt 1998; Vahabzadeh 2009; Williams 2000).

Through the works of Merleau-Ponty (2000[1962], 1968), a critique levelled at this ontological separation of the mind and body is that, existentially, we are our bodies. Our material existence dictates the way we think about the world and for Merleau-Ponty this stands in opposition to the supposed objectivity of positivism and scientific empiricism which assumes the existence of dichotomies between the observer and observed, and the subject and the object. Rather than view perception as a passive process, Merleau-Ponty argues that it is an active, reflexive process that contests these dichotomies. Individuals learn via the body, and through somatic movements, they "revise [their] notion of 'understand' and [their] notion of the body" (Merleau-Ponty 2000, 144). The mind and body are closely intertwined and ontologically inseparable because "we have no idea of a mind that would not be doubled with a body, that would not be established on this ground" (1968, 259). Damasio (1994, 233) argues that this bifurcation between the mind and body is impossible because motor and somatosensory systems are simultaneously engaged in decision-making processes and that "feelings are a powerful influence on reason" (1994, 245). LeDoux (1996, 37) elucidates how this rational/ irrational distinction is not a boundary since cognition and emotions are closely intertwined such that "emotional feelings result when we become consciously aware that an emotion system of the brain is active" (1996, 302). LeDoux (2002) cites fear conditioning, a process where organisms use fear as a mechanism to make a rational decision as an example.

The body is a site of mnemonic importance, and enshrined within the body are particular ways of knowing and experiencing. In addition, the body, being the mode by which individuals come to perceive the world, allows one to experience temporality and spatiality. The ways by which individuals come to know and think of their bodies are thus the result of different socio-historical moments. Embodiment provides not only an alternative framework to deconstruct issues such as culture, gender, and power (Csordas 1994a, b; 1999) but also a means to analyse different socio-historical milieux.

In addition, meaning is generated through bodies and sensory percep-tions, emerging via somatic movements, feel, and the sensory feedback from other bodies (Nancy 2000, 2008). Nancy (2008, 153) argues:

> ... bodies cross paths, rub up and press against each other, embrace or col-lide with one another: they send each other all these signals, so many signals, addresses, notices, which no defined sense can exhaust. Bodies produce a sense beyond sense. They're an extravagance of sense. Which is why a body seems to assume its sense only once it's dead, fixed. And maybe why we interpret the body as the soul's tomb. In reality, a body never stops stirring. Death freezes the movement of letting go and declining to stir.

Furthering the phenomenological project, Nancy argues for recognising the importance of other senses aside from sight and touch. However, this knowledge is always fragmented because of our interpretative schemes (Ricoeur 1974) that limit the way we perceive the world, our inability to know what others are experiencing. In addressing my research problematic of why the men choose to train in Thailand and what they get out of their training, a phenomenological approach, where the researcher's bodily experiences is intertwined with the everyday gym's regimes, necessitates understanding how particular circumstances give rise to different somatic understandings/experiences of the body and the creation of a liminal space at the gym. Bodies can be constantly reinvented, "a phenomenological habitus that is a lived-through structure-in-process continually amenable to changes" (Spencer 2012, 32). Rather than focus simply on how habitus relates to one's cultural and socio-economic biographies (cf. Bourdieu 1977, 1990a, b), I pay attention to how the men talk about their own personal martial arts habitus vis-à-vis their bodies and senses.

SPORTING BODIES AND MASCULINITIES

Sport is a pedagogical tool that socialises individuals into societal mores and norms, and facilitates character-building by inculcating in individuals values such as discipline, commitment, dedication, sacrifice, and fortitude (Butcher and Schneider 2001). Through sports such as rugby and football, academics analyse various cultural components such as issues of performance (Blackshaw and Crabbe 2004; Rinchart 1998), identity formation (Curry 2000; Kohn 2003), and national identity (Archetti and Dyck 2003; Klein 1997; Ots 2003). A recurrent theme across these different cultural aspects is that of sports as associated with the perpetuation and reproduction of gender hierarchies (Messner and Sabo 1994; Pronger 2000). Connell's (1995) theory of hegemonic masculinity critically deconstructs the previously static conceptualisation of gender and argues that masculinities need to be situated both temporally and spatially. Hegemonic masculinity is:

> ...not a fixed entity embedded in the body or personality traits of individuals...masculinities are configurations of practice that are accomplished in social action, and therefore, can differ according to gender relations in a particular social setting (Connell and Messerschmidt 2005, 836).

This dynamic conceptualisation of gender requires a contextualisation of how various dimensions of social life result in a particular manifestation of masculinities. Connell's theory allows for the existence of multiple forms of masculinities and for the fact that hegemonic masculinity is constantly in flux and open to challenge. The maintenance of a hierarchy of masculinities necessitates the subordination and marginalisation of men who embody these non-dominant forms.

Furthering Connell and Messerschmidt's (2005, 841) theoretical contribution in pointing out how men situationally adopt hegemonic masculinities, academics have furnished a more nuanced understanding of masculinity vis-à-vis the sociology of the everyday life and the body (cf. Alter 1992; Whitson 1990). In this book, I utilise a phenomenological approach to analyse the everyday realities of fighters and what they get out of doing martial arts. I pay attention to how fighters subscribe to and attempt to embody a particular version of hegemonic masculinity, and the sanctions applied against those who fail to conform. For these men, the somatic performance of masculinities is not only one of the key components of being a fighter but part of the gym's culture. Once at the gym, men are interpellated into this hierarchy whether they want it or not and performing the accepted version of masculinity is through demonstrating one's willingness to fight and the ability gracefully to accept defeat. Individuals, who do not subscribe to this morality or competitive element, will thus be marginalised. In addition, a different yardstick of what constitutes rationality applies at the gym, as individuals subject their bodies to particular regimes that from an ethic perspective might be considered irrational.

Chapters' Outline

In my introductory chapter, I have drawn upon an eclectic body of literature to understand the phenomenon of foreigners travelling to Thailand to learn martial arts. The centrality of the body in the transmission of bodily techniques and perpetuation of somatic cultures underscores my research problematic of how culture impacts the way individuals think about and utilise their bodies. In Chap. 2, I shall discuss how the gym's isolated location has an appeal for foreigners who deliberately choose not to train at mainstream, commercialised gyms. To comprehend these emic perspectives, I articulate the need for an embodied methodology, a methodological approach that not only sees me training, living, and interacting with the men daily within a communal setting but also sensitises me to the need for a phenomenological analysis. My own personal biography as a martial artist allowed me to establish rapport with these martial arts aficionados and my fieldwork, entailing an intimate involvement in their lives, provided some insights into the motivations and goals that drove them to take time off to train in martial arts.

In Chap. 3, I outline the ideal life of a disciplined fighter. I describe the physical layout of the gym in order to ground this ethnographic study empirically. I depict the somatic and masculine gym culture as experienced through the men's everyday lives and the ways in which the various aspects of their lives, from dietary to lifestyle restrictions, are regulated and disciplined. From these regimes, the men gain a heightened somatic awareness of their bodies and a more muscular, agile body that has been conditioned to stand up to the rigours of martial combat. Elias's (2000) concept of the "civilising process" forms this chapter's theoretical framework. I argue that in order to be fighters, the men need to put aside their inhibitions of the civilising process. Together with the gym's structural isolation, this creates an embodied liminality for the men. In Chap. 4, I continue this thread of exploring embodied experiences. Focusing on bodily frames of behaviour to situate the acquisition of bodily knowledge, I first articulate the sensory reconfiguration that a fighter has to undergo if he wishes to be successful. Next, I analyse how the aging body and the harsh punishments to which the men subject their bodies impact bodily frames of behaviour. Through their embodied narratives, I highlight some of the ramifications these processes have on their continued quest to be martial artists.

In Chap. 5, I move beyond the confines of the gym and examine how transnational flows impact the discursive construction and practice of martial arts. The flow of individuals, televised images and particular techniques of the body (Mauss 2006) across transnational boundaries results in individuals drawing upon an eclectic array of martial disciplines that in turn impact the transmission and modification of sensorial knowledge. Locating commercial interests as one of the driving forces behind the global spread of martial arts, I briefly examine the impact commercialisation has had on the development of martial arts and the men's reactions towards the banal commercialisation process. In my concluding chapter, I highlight the two recurrent themes of this somatic culture, the phenomenological element and the layered rationality that exists. The latter refers to how the men subject their bodies to seemingly contradictory practices that may seem irrational from an etic perspective. I also discuss how their experiences at the gym influenced their bodily dispositions and outlook towards life.

REFERENCES

Alexander, R. (2009). Globalisation and the 'Internal Alchemy' in Chinese Martial Arts: The transmission of Taijiquan to Britain. *East Asia Science, Technology and Society: An International Journal, 2*(1), 525–543.

Alter, J. S. (1992). *The Wrestler's body. Identity and ideology in North India.* Berkeley: University of California Press.

Alter, J. S. (2002). Pehlwani: Indian wrestling and somatic nationalism. In D. E. Jones (Ed.), *Combat, ritual, and performance. Anthropology of the martial arts.* London: Praeger.

Archetti, E. P., & Dyck, N. (2003). Playing football and dancing tango: Embodying Argentina in movement, style and identity. In E. P. Archetti & N. Dyck (Eds.), *Dance, sport and embodied masculinities.* Oxford: Berg Press.

Ashkenazi, M. (2002). Ritual and the ideal of society in karate. In D. E. Jones (Ed.), *Combat, ritual, and performance. Anthropology of the martial arts.* London: Praeger.

Atkinson, M. (2008). Exploring male femininity in the 'crisis': Men and cosmetic surgery. *Body and Society, 14*(1), 67–97.

Bangkok Post. (2008, August 6). Muay Thai-conquest to rule the world reaping results. *Bangkok Post.*

Berger, Peter L. *The Sacred Canopy: Elements of a Sociology of Religion.* New York: Anchor Books; 1967.

Blackshaw, T., & Crabbe, T. (2004). *New perspectives on sport and 'deviance': Consumption, performativity and social control.* London: Routledge.

Bohwongprasert, Y. (2003, February 2). Muay Thai making progress in leaps and bounds around the world. *Bangkok Post.*

Bourdieu, P. (1977). *Outline of a theory of practice* (R. Nice, Trans.). Cambridge: Cambridge University Press.

Bourdieu, P. (1990a). *The logic of practice.* Stanford, CA: Stanford University Press.

Bourdieu, P. (1990b). *In other words: Essays towards a reflexive sociology* (M. Adamson, Trans.). Stanford, CA: Stanford University Press.

Brown, J., & Graham, D. (2008). Body satisfaction in gym-active males: An exploration of sexuality, gender and narcissism. *Sex Roles, 59*(1–2), 94–106.

Bryson, L. (1990). Sport, drug and the development of modern capitalism. *Sporting Traditions, 6*(2), 135–153.

Burkitt, I. (1998). Bodies of knowledge: Beyond Cartesian views of persons, selves, and mind. *Journal for the Theory of Social Behaviour, 32*(2), 219–237.

Butcher, R. B., & Schneider, A. J. (2001). Fair play as respect for the game. In W. J. Morgan, K. V. Meier, & A. J. Schneider (Eds.), *Ethics in sports.* Champaign: Human Kinetics.

Connell, R. W. (1995). *Masculinities.* Berkeley: University of California Press.

Connell, R. W., & Messerschmidt, J. W. (2005). Hegemonic masculinity: Rethinking the concept. *Gender and Society, 19*(6), 829–859.

Crossley, N. (1995). Merleau-Ponty, the elusive body and carnal sociology. *Body and Society, 1*(1), 43–63.

Crossley, N. (1996). *Intersubjectivity. The fabric of social becoming*. London: Sage.

Crossley, N. (2006). In the gym motives, meanings and moral careers. *Body and Society, 12*(3), 25–50.

Crossley, N. (2007). Researching embodiment by way of 'body techniques'. In C. Shilling (Ed.), *Embodying sociology: Retrospect, progress and prospects*. Malden, MA: Blackwell.

Csordas, T. J. (1994a). Introduction: The body as representation and being-in-the-world. In T. J. Csordas (Ed.), *Embodiment and experience: The existential ground of culture and self*. Cambridge: Cambridge University Press.

Csordas, T. J. (1994b). Words from the holy people: A case study in cultural phenomenology. In T. J. Csordas (Ed.), *Embodiment and experience: The existential ground of culture and self*. Cambridge: Cambridge University Press.

Csordas, T. J. (1999). Embodiment and cultural phenomenology. In G. Weiss & H. F. Haber (Eds.), *Perspectives on embodiment: The intersections of nature and culture*. New York: Routledge.

Curry, T. J. (2000). Booze and barfights: A journey to the dark side of college athletics. In J. McKay, M. A. Messner, & D. F. Sabo (Eds.), *Masculinities, gender relations, and sport*. London: Sage Publication.

Damasio, A. R. (1994). *Descartes' error. Emotion, reason and the human brain*. New York: A Grosset/Putnam Book.

Delamont, S., & Stephens, N. (2006). Balancing the berimbau Qualitative Inquiry, Vol 12, No 2.

Delamont, S., & Stephens, N. (2008). Up on the roof: The embodied habitus of Diasporic Capoeira. *Cultural Sociology, 2*(1), 57–74.

Descartes, R. (1998)[1641]. *Discourse on method and the meditations*. London: Penguin.

Donohue, J. J. (1991). *The forge of the spirit: Structure, motion and meaning in the Japanese Martial Tradition*. New York: Garland Publications.

Donohue, J. J. (1994a). *The martial arts and the American imagination*. West Port, CT: Bergin and Garvey.

Donohue, J. J. (1994b). *Warrior dreams: The martial arts and the American imagination*. West Port, CT: Bergin and Garvey.

Donohue, J. J. (2002). Wave people: The martial arts and the American imagination. Combat, ritual, and performance. In D. E. Jones (Ed.), *Anthropology of the martial arts*. London: Praeger.

Downey, G. (2007). Producing pain: Techniques and technologies in no-holds-barred fighting. *Social Studies of Science, 37*(2), 201–226.

Elias, N. (2000). The civilising process. In: E. Dunning, J. Goudsblom, & S. Mennell (Eds.), *Sociogenetic and psychogentic investigations* (E. Jephcott, Trans.). Cornwall: Blackwell.

Farnell, B. (1999). Moving bodies, acting selves. *Annual Review Anthropology*, 28(1), 341–373.

Farrer, D. S. (2009). *Shadows of the prophet: Martial arts and Sufi mysticism.* In G. Marranci & B. S. Turner (Eds.), Muslims in Global Societies Series Volume 2. Dordrecht: Springer

Featherstone, M. (2007). *Consumer culture and postmodernism* (2nd ed.). Thousand Oaks, CA: Sage.

Frank, A. W. (1991). For a sociology of the body: An analytical review. In M. Featherstone, M. Hepworth, & B. S. Turner (Eds.), *The body: Social processes and cultural theory.* London: Sage.

Garcia, R. S., & Malcom, D. (2010). Decivillizing, civilizing or informalizing? The international development of mixed martial arts. *International Review for the Sociology of Sport*, 45(1), 39–58.

Gibson, J. J. (1979). *The ecological approach to visual perception.* Boston: Houghton Miflin.

Giddens, A. (1991). *Modernity and self-identity: Self and society in the late modern age.* Palo Alto, CA: Stanford University Press.

Glogower, N. B. (2009). *A good defence will leave you beautiful. A Bad Defence will make you Ugly.* Gender in Muay Thai Kickboxing. Master's Thesis. America: University of Michigan.

Green, T. A., & Svinth, J. R. (Eds.). (2003). *Martial arts in the modern world.* London: Praeger.

Hockey, J., & Allen-Collinson, J. (2009). The sensorium at work: The sensory phenomenology of the working body. *The Sociological Review*, 57(2), 217–39.

Holcombe, C. (2002). Theatre of combat: A critical look at the Chinese Martial Arts. In T. A. Green & J. R. Svinth (Eds.), *Combat, ritual, and performance. Anthropology of the martial arts.* London: Praeger.

Honkasalo, M.-L. (1998). Space and embodied experience: Rethinking the body in pain. *Body and Society*, 4(2), 35–57.

Howson, A., & Inglis, D. (2001). The body in sociology: Tensions inside and outside sociological thought. *Sociological Review*, 49(3), 297–317.

Husserl, E. (1960)[1931]. *Cartesian meditations.* The Hague, The Netherlands: Nijhoff.

Jone, D. E. (Ed.). (2002). *Combat, ritual, and performance. Anthropology of the martial arts.* London: Praeger.

Junlakan, L., & Prayukvong, K. (2001). *Muay Thai: A living legacy.* Bangkok: Spry.

Katz, J., & Csordas, T. J. (2003). Phenomenological ethnography in sociology and anthropology. *Ethnography*, 4(3), 275–288.

Klein, A. M. (1997). *Baseball on the border: A tale of two Laredos.* Princeton, New Jersey: Princeton University.

Kohn, T. (2003). The Aikido body: Expressions of group identities and self-discovery in martial arts training. In E. P. Archetti & N. Dyck (Eds.), *Dance, sport, and embodied identities*. Oxford: Berg.

Konig, E. (1995). Criticism of doping: The Nihilistic side of technological sport and the antiquated view of sport ethics. *International Review for the Sociology of Sport, 34*(3/4), 247–261.

LeDoux, J. (1996). *The emotional brain: The mysterious underpinnings of emotional life*. Atlanta, GA: Simon and Schuster.

LeDoux, J. (2002). *Synaptic self: How our brains become who we are*. Harmondsworth, England: Viking Penguin.

Lee, W. (2009). Jurus, Jazz Riffs and the constitution of a national martial art in Indonesia. *Body and Society, 15*(3), 93–119.

Loh, H.L.L. (2010). *Transcending dichotomies: Embodied intersections of self, structure and agency amongst Singaporean Chinese males*. Academic Exercise-Department of Sociology, Faculty of Arts and Social Sciences, Singapore: National University of Singapore.

Loh, L. H. (2011). Cultural myths: Unpacking the origins of Muay Thai. *Journal of Asian Martial Arts, 20*(3), 32–37.

Mauss, M. (2006)[1935]. Techniques of the body. In: N. Schlanger (Ed., Introduced) *Techniques, technology and civilisation*. New York: Durkheim Press.

Mellor, P. A., & Shilling, C. (1997). *Re-forming the body: Religion, community and modernity*. London: Sage.

Merleau-Ponty, M. (1968). *The visible and the invisible: Followed by working notes*. Evanston, IL: Northwestern University Press.

Merleau-Ponty, M. (2000)[1962]. *Phenomenology of perception* (6th ed.) (C. Smith, Trans., with translation revisions supplied by Forrest Williams and David Guerriere). London: Routledge and Kegan Paul.

Messner, M. A., & Sabo, D. F. (1994). *Sex, violence, and power in sports*. Freedom: California, Crossing Press.

Moustakas, C. (1994). *Phenomenological research method*. Thousand Oaks, CA: Sage.

Nancy, J. L. (2000). *Being singular plural*. Stanford, CA: Stanford University Press.

Nancy, J. L. (2008). *Corpus*. New York: Fordham University Press.

Norjidi, D. (2009, September 18). Brunei reaches new level in Muay Thai. *Borneo Bulletin*. Brunei: Brunei Press Sdn Bhd.

Nur Amali, I. (2001). *Ringside stories: Lives, experiences and identities of Muay Thai boxers*. Academic Exercise-Department of Southeast Asia Studies, Faculty of Arts and Social Sciences, Singapore: National University of Singapore.

Ots, T. (2003). The silenced body—The expressive Leib: On the dialectic of mind and life in Chinese cathartic healing. In T. Csordas (Ed.), *Embodiment and experience: The existential ground of culture and self.* Cambridge: Cambridge University Press.

Pattana, K. (2005). Lives of hunting dogs' Muay Thai and the politics of Thai masculinities. *South East Asia Research, 13*(1), 57–90.

Pattana, K. (2007). *Muay Thai cinemas and the burdens of Thai men* (Working Paper Series, Asia Research Institute 88). Singapore: National University of Singapore.

Pronger, B. (2000). Homosexuality and sport: Who's Winning. In J. McKay, M. A. Messner, & D. F. Sabo (Eds.), *Masculinities, gender relations, and sport.* London: Sage Publication.

Ricoeur, R. (1974). Existence and hermeneutics. In D. Ihde (Ed.), *The conflict of interpretations.* Evanston, IL: Northwestern University Press.

Rinchart, R. (1998). *Players all: Performances in contemporary sport.* Bloomington: Indiana University Press.

Satterlund, T. D. (2006). *Fighting for an authentic self: An ethnographic study of recreational boxers.* Unpublished doctoral thesis, University of North Carolina, North Carolina.

Schutz, A. (1967). *The phenomenology of the social world.* Evanston, IL: Northwestern University Press.

Shahar, M. (2008). *The Shaolin monastery: History, religion and the Chinese Martial Arts.* Honolulu: University of Hawaii Press.

Shilling, C. (1993). *The body and social theory.* London, Newbury Park: Sage.

Shilling, C. (2007). Sociology and the body: Classical traditions and new agenda. In C. Shilling (Ed.), *Embodying sociology: Retrospect, progress and prospects.* United Kingdom: Blackwell.

Shilling, C. (2008). *Changing bodies. Habit, crisis and creativity.* London: Sage.

Spencer, D. C. (2009). Habit(us), body techniques and body callusing: An ethnography of mixed martial arts. *Body and Society, 15*(4), 119–143.

Spencer, D. C. (2012). *Ultimate fighting and embodiment. Violence, gender, and mixed martial arts.* New York: Routledge.

Tan, S. Y. K. (2008). *Bodies of culture, history and power in the practice of Aikido in Canada.* Unpublished doctoral thesis, University of Alberta, Canada.

Thai News Service. (2011, January 26). Thailand: Move to promote Muay Thai as an International Sport. *Thai News Service.*

Toh, S. K. (2002). *Kicking the Thai out of the Muay: An exploratory study of Thai Kickboxing in Singapore.* National University of Singapore: Academic Exercise-Department of Sociology, Faculty of Arts and Social Sciences, Singapore.

Turner, S. B. (1984). *The body and society.* New York: Basil Blackwell.

Tuxill, C., & Wigmore, S. (1991). Cheating the public? An exploration of some issues surrounding the condemnation of the use of drugs in sport. *Physical Education Review, 14*(2), 119–128.

Vahabzadeh, P. (2009). Ultimate referentiality: Radical phenomenology and the new interpretative sociology. *Philosophy and Social Criticism, 35*(4), 447–465.

Vail, P. (1998). Modern Muay Thai mythology. *Crossroads: An Interdisciplinary Journal of Southeast Asia Studies, 12*(2), 75–95.

Van Bottenburg, M., & Heilbron, J. (2006). De-sportization of fighting contests: The origins and dynamics of no holds barred events and the theory of sportization. *International Review for the Sociology of Sports, 41*(3), 259–282.

Van Wolputte, S. (2004). Hang on to your self: Of bodies, embodiment, and selves. *Annual Review of Anthropology, 33*(1), 251–69.

Voy, R. (1991). *Drugs, sport and politics.* Champaign: Leisure Press.

Wacquant, L. (1995). The pugilistic point of view: How boxers think and feel about their trade. *Theory and Society, 24*(1), 489–535.

Wacquant, L. (1998). A Fleshpeddler at work: Power, pain, and profit in the prize-fighting economy. *Theory and Society, 27*(1), 1–42.

Wacquant, L. (2004). *Body and soul, notebooks of an apprentice boxer.* Oxford: Oxford University Press.

Wacquant, L. (2005). Carnal connections: On embodiment, apprenticeship, and membership. *Qualitative Sociology, 28*(4), 445–474.

Whitson, D. (1990). Sport and the social construction of masculinity. In M. A. Messner & D. F. Sabo (Eds.), *Sport, men, and the gender order: Critical feminist perspectives.* Champain, IL: Human Kinetics.

Williams, S. (2000). Reason, emotion and embodiment: Is mental health a contradiction in terms? *Sociology of Health and Illness, 22*(5), 559–581.

Yip, W. Y. (2011, September 22). Muay Thai with more punch. *The Strait Times.* Singapore: Singapore Press Holdings.

Zarrilli, P. B. (1998). *When the body becomes all eyes. Paradigms, discourses and practices of power in Kalarippayattu, a South Indian martial art.* Delhi: Oxford University Press.

CHAPTER 2

Methodology

Abstract This methodology chapter provides the context and social reality of the field site. The embodied nature of martial arts necessitates a methodology where there is a need to the need "to deploy the body as a tool of inquiry and vector of knowledge" (Wacquant, L. (2004). *Body and Soul, Notebooks of an Apprentice Boxer.* Oxford: Oxford University Press), "go native armed" (Wacquant, L. (2009). Habitus as topic and tool: reflections on becoming a prizefighter. In W. Shaffir, A. Puddephatt, S. Kleinknecht (Eds.) *Ethnographies Revisited,* New York: Routledge). As an ethnographer, I delineate some of the conceptual, methodological and ethical concerns that underpin this study and discuss the various ways in which the sensorial and bodily sensations experienced by these martial artists can be comprehended and translated for the benefit of an academic audience.

For 5 weeks, I embedded myself in the social reality of Kwaan-saa-maat Gym [Might Gym], a Muay Thai and MMA gym, in Ubon Ratchathani, Thailand, training, living, and interacting with the other participants at the gym. As accommodation is provided for, everyone stays and trains at the gym, making this field site one that is geographically bounded. Following Gore's (1999) argument that representational practices inform and imbue all aspects of fieldwork, I am aware that the field exists not as an empirical but conceptual space. What constitutes a field needs to be problematised

© The Editor(s) (if applicable) and The Author(s) 2016
Loh H.L.L, *The Body and Senses in Martial Culture,*
DOI 10.1057/978-1-137-55742-1_2

precisely because sites are imbued with a historical dimension and are interpreted through the subjectivity and positionality of the researcher (Buckland
1999; Grau 1999; Tedlock 2000). Representations of the field define the
modalities in which martial arts is construed since "field and culture are
often conceived as coterminous in several if not in all their dimensions"
(Gore 1999, 210). While there are numerous martial arts gyms, owned
by both Thais and foreigners abound in places such as Bangkok, Phuket,
Chiang Mai, and Koh Samui, I deliberately chose Kwaan-saa-maat Gym
because of its relative isolation, situated far beyond these touristy locations.
The rural province of Ubon Ratachathani is an hour's flight away from
Bangkok. Other than those who come to train in martial arts, Ubon, an
agricultural and rural province, rarely attracts foreigners. Unsurprisingly,
individuals at the gym often attempt to differentiate themselves from other
non-Thais by vocalising their disdain for the idea of training at gyms located
near tourist hot spots. They prefer to subject themselves to the more stren-
uous martial arts training at Kwaan-saa-maat Gym which is of a variety not
found at those gyms. Michael is a Norwegian student, aged 18. His comment typifies the kind of responses given by the participants when asked
why they decide to come all the way to rural Thailand to train:

> How I heard about Kwaan-saa-maat Gym? I just googled it and type Issan
> and Muay Thai. I wanted to get away from everything and Issan is far enough,
> away from tourist traps! At the World Muay Thai Council at Koh Samui, it is
> much more tourist focused… they don't push you as hard like here…

A particular appeal of Kwaan-saa-maat Gym is the opportunity to train
with its owner, described by Stefan, 22, a German student, as being "one
of the top Muay Thai fighters. He was actually one of the best in the
world!" Another is the lack of distractions due to Kwaan-saa-maat Gym's
location far away from popular tourist destinations. Karl, 22, a Scottish
postgraduate, explains why it appeals to him:

> I also wanted to get out of way from the touristy place like Pattaya, Phuket,
> Koh Samui, it's just too much distractions. Too hectic and all. I wanted to
> be out here where it's relaxed. Hectic as in it is just partying and people
> hustling you? It is just more stressful. More traffic, more bars that people
> go to, girls, so many things to distract you, put you off Muay Thai. Cheap
> alcohol, the beaches and stuff. Out here there is less to do, enough to keep
> you entertained but you just train and that is what you do. Don't get to do
> anything else except train so it is good that way.

Martial arts gyms in Thailand that cater to foreigners constitute a transient community. Most individuals, with the exception of the instructors, stay at the gym from between a week to a few months. Prior to my trip, I liaised with the owner of Kwaan-saa-maat Gym and obtained his consent to conduct my fieldwork there. Throughout my entire stay at Kwaan-saa-maat Gym, I became acquainted with 22 men, the majority coming from Scandinavian countries like Sweden and Norway. Excluding the Thai Muay Thai instructors, there were only three other Asians there during my stay. These men are mainly in their early 20s; the youngest is 18 and the oldest 39. Coming from diverse occupations, from law undergraduate to security guard, one commonality they share is their socio-economic status. Most of the participants are of at least a middle-class background and so are able to afford the opportunity costs of training in Thailand for a prolonged period of time without worrying about their means of livelihood (see Appendix A). I was informed that it is very rare for women to come and train at the gym.

Manson (2002, 17) delineates the linkages between a particular research topic and its relation to the researcher's ontological and epistemological positions and how this is reflective of one's own biography. My biography as an avid martial arts practitioner who has practised Aikido, a Japanese form of self-defence, for more than 8 years fuelled my interest in this academic inquiry. Sensitised by Wacquant's (2004) *Body and Soul, Notebooks of an Apprentice Boxer*, the need to "to deploy the body as a tool of inquiry and vector of knowledge" (Wacquant 2004, viii), "go native armed" (Wacquant 2009, 8), and the need to prepare myself with the necessary sporting/bodily capital, I signed up for classes at a Singapore Muay Thai gym to acquaint myself with the somatic movements of Muay Thai and to acquire the necessary martial arts "legitimacy" before embarking on my fieldwork. Given how the presentation of the self/body (Goffman 1971) has ramifications for establishing my credentials and social survival within the field, the primary identity that I performed is that of a martial artist, being involved in the gym's everyday routines and regimes. This is reflected in both the way I participated in the gym's daily activities and the ability to demonstrate an insider's knowledge when certain questions are levelled at me. The extract below, where I consciously elected to prioritise the name of my gym over my nationality, highlights my strategic use of identities:

Wan, 33, Canadian, professional fighter: So where are you from?

L.L   Oh I train at Impact MMA back in Singapore.

Wan   Cool! Impact! I heard of that place. They have a branch in Hong Kong, right?

To reiterate, this is a conscious stratagem to conform to this social milieu and establish rapport with the participants.

Later, when I disclosed the fact that I am also doing an academic research on Muay Thai, the guys were often surprised that their passion, martial arts, can be studied within an academic context. Many were extremely receptive to the idea, often volunteering their time to be interviewed and even expressing interest in my research's progress. Our shared enthusiasm for martial arts not only helped to establish rapport but also greatly facilitated the research process. To concretely establish the fact that my passion for martial arts does not solely exist within the discursive realms of academia, I actively participated in the daily training sessions and non-obligatory runs that take place before each training sessions, demonstrating to the men that I am not simply an academic. As my cardiovascular stamina and skills began to improve, the others started to remember my name and became more receptive to my presence. The importance of involving my body in the rigours of training paid off when Jack, 22, an unemployed Swedish man, who despite visiting Thailand for the first time, decided to stay for 2 months at Kwaan-saa-maat Gym, commented:

> I really like you doing so hard exercises even though you are here for schoolwork. You are trying hard, you are really doing the best you can! For me, it's more important to do what you can do. That impresses me more if someone pushes himself to his limits, than [if] I see a really good fighter, doing some pro job but not pushing yourself. It doesn't inspire me as much.

Conversely, Peder, 22, another unemployed Swede, who does not often train with the guys and lazes in his room, is subjected to constant ridicule and contempt:

James	So where were you yesterday man? We didn't see you around.
Peder	I was at Peppers [a restaurant selling predominantly western cuisine].
Jack	Yesterday was sparring... you wouldn't see Peder there man! [laughs]
Peder	Yeah, I don't like getting hit but I will be the Ultimate Fighting Champion (UFC) in 5 years.
Wan	[laughs] You are not going to get better by avoiding it man... you have an ego...

These extracts highlight how this community is only accessible via the currency of sweat, toil, and bruises gained through training. Kwaan-saa-maat Gym is the site where a community of individuals coming from diverse cultures and nationalities are united in their passion for martial arts, subjugating their bodies to the rigours of training. The men often refer to each other as "the guys" and this becomes part of a shared and cohesive identity. Communal moments are created when the guys talk about the fights they have seen or participated in. In addition, the training grounds have a dual functionality: they are at the same time a site where bodies get reconfigured as particular martial disciplines become embodied, and just a place to hang out. This sense of *communitas* is exemplified by Veron, 28, Indian, unemployed, who comments:

> Aside from discipline and focus, meeting up with amazing people, amazing fighters and understanding their reasons for fighting and learning Muay Thai is also impressive. People come from all walks of life, there are electricians, there are street fighters, there are university graduates who learn Muay Thai. So you try understanding what works for them [and that] inspire[s] me... these are people who have a past and they decided to channel their energies, channel their focus in the right way. In doing something good in their life, they focus on Muay Thai.

Turner (1696) conceptualises communitas as existential or spontaneous social groups that are forged through a sense of collective purpose, communion, and emotional bonds. As the above extract demonstrates, the shared experiences of the participants engaging in martial arts training allow them to transcend their socio-structural positions and nationalities and focus on martial arts.

In addition to training and interacting with the participants on the premises of the gym, I joined them on their leisurely excursions to places such as Swensens, the ice-cream parlour in town, the local zoo, clubs, and pubs. I also went with them to watch local Muay Thai matches in Ubon and MMA matches in Bangkok. The time spent at all these places yielded useful data. In particular, being in attendance at martial arts matches meant that not only can I witness some of the guys fight professionally, but it also allowed me the privilege of listening to the comments they made in response to the ongoing social drama, which are reflective of their own repository of embodied knowledge.

Given the complexity of experiencing and documenting somatic cultures and knowledge, I utilised (1) performance ethnography, (2) semi-structured in-depth interviewing, and (3) photo elicitation to uncover the motivations behind my participants' desire to invest time and money in martial arts and how their physicality has changed as a result.

PERFORMANCE ETHNOGRAPHY AND THE SENSES

Researchers on somatic cultures such as dance and martial arts often stress the materiality of the body as being central to understanding the lived realities of these practices, given that language alone is often inadequate to convey and transmit embodied knowledge (Leigh Foster 2003; Potter 2008; Samudra 2008). Practice, constituted by "shared skills and understanding," "tacit knowledge," and "embodied, materially mediated arrays of human activity" (Schatzki et al. 2000, 2–3), is thus central to my research methodology. A number of similar generic terminologies are often used for this, such as "performance ethnography," "practice-as-research," and "performance as research." In their review of the methodologies used in theatre and performance studies, Kershaw et al. (2011, 63–65) argue that "practice-as-research," which is characterised by "post-binary commitment to activity (rather than structure), process (rather than fixity), action (rather than representation), collectiveness (rather than individualism), and reflexivity (rather than self-consciousness)," untangles the ontology/epistemology binary, the "unsustainable bifurcations between becoming and being." As embodied knowledge is not easily transmitted except through learning a skill for yourself, this methodology attempts to bridge the chasm between "practical" and "discursive" consciousness. Polanyi (1983, 10) argues that this form of tacit knowing, whereby one knows proximal (practical consciousness) only by attending to the distal (discursive consciousness), reflects how individuals "can know more than we can tell" (1983, 4). For Giddens (1984, 49), the former refers to "recall to which the agent has access in the durée of action without being able to express what he or she thereby 'knows'", while the latter refers to "recall which the actor is able to express verbally." In short, while an individual is able to perform a particular physical action, he may lack the vocabulary to articulate or translate this physical performance into words. I will later elaborate what implications this methodology has for the politics of representation and writing.

Performance ethnography, as an embodied methodology, allows research to be conducted about and through bodies due to the embodied sensuous experiences that "create the conditions for understanding... [P] erformed experiences are the sites where felt emotion, memory, desire and understanding come together" (Denzin 2003, 13). Performance ethnography allows the researcher to comprehend how meanings are associated, perpetuated, and sustained through movements, how the subjective framing by cultural evaluation and intention of a particular event gives rise to meanings, and the motivations behind which particular movements are generated, and a yardstick by which to contextualise and situate these movements. Kaeppler (1999, 22) cautions against marginalising the role of the audience because "movement sequences are analogous to utterances, and without knowledge of the movement conventions, a viewer will be unable to understand what is being conveyed." This methodology reiterates Kaeppler's (1999) advice because it captures the ongoing dynamics between the performer and audience. As a methodology in which my material body is intrinsically intertwined with the ongoing social processes, performance ethnography allows for the construction of experiential knowledge vis-à-vis my subjective experiences, observations, and perceptions (Dickson-Swift et al. 2009; Okley 2007; Parker-Starbuck and Mock 2011; Seymour 2007). The visual, verbal, sensual, olfactory, and kinaesthetic processes at the gym are all important sources of data, generated by subjecting my body to the rigours of the gym, by bodies interacting and communicating in social drama that unfolds, at times, non-verbally. The way in which our senses are directed to perceive selective aspects of reality is influenced by one's cultural, ontological, and epistemological paradigms (Howes 2003; Howes 2004a, b), and self-reflexivity, on the part of the researcher, is necessary to translate that which is experiential, and interpretive onto the discursive dimension. Within this somatic culture, my body is "a tool of inquiry and vector for knowledge" (Wacquant 2004, viii):

> Already, bruises are starting to form on my right shin, the leg that I frequently use to execute roundhouse kicks. In a sense, I am modifying my body, making some parts of it, deemed by the martial arts community as essential to fighting, stronger and faster. I commented to Ivar, 39, Swede, security guard, whose shin is a whole mass of bruises how hardcore he is. He smiled and said, "At least you know you are hitting the right places."

Fieldnotes 11 September 2011

My body functions as a tool to analyse the interpretative practices (Gubrium and Holstein 2000) at the gym by adhering to the specific somatic practices. Bodily experiences can be indexed against the way in which individuals systematically construct their worldview, and the configurations of shared understanding, rituals, and practices at the gym.

In addition, Green (2011), in his ethnographic study of the lives of MMA fighters, discusses how his informants, after engaging in sparring sessions, are often eager to talk to their sparring partners about their experiences and feelings. Corresponding to Green's (2011) findings, I too realised the transformative element of sparring as individuals are often eager to reflect on and talk about their experiences. I capitalised on this and attempted to inquire about their experiences in the interviews or to use our shared experiences as a starting point from which to probe further. Performance ethnography also sensitises me to the affective element that arises during training. By affect, I am referring to the "continuous nonconscious self-perception" that occurs as a "background perception that accompanies every event, however, quotidian" (Massumi 2002, 35–36), the emotions and feelings experienced. The interview transcript below illustrates these points:

L.L   How do you counter Jack's reach? I am still thinking about every time I spar with him and Jack just goes hard on you right?

Aaron, 27, American, undergraduate: Yeah he goes hard! I got it man! I figured it out yesterday. You got to slip. He throws a lot of jabs man! He knows how to use his reach. So you got to time his jabs, where you can time his jabs, you slip this way? [moves his torso towards one direction] And you go to the body man! [throws a couple of punches at the level of my torso and I unconsciously raise my guard in response] And that makes him drop his hands? So you go to the body and you go to his face [thows punches at my face level]. And whenever he gets hit in the body man he freaks out! He just stands there and you can just boom, boom, boom [rapidly throwing punches to the torso and face level]. So watch for the jabs, slip the jabs, body, head and then you fucking got him man! [laughs]

L.L   Thanks for the tip man! [I start to mirror Aaron's actions of weaving my body and jabbing at the torso and then the head]

This extract highlights the usefulness of drawing upon shared experiences as an interview probe, the affective element that occurs not only during training but as participants attempt to verbalise their thoughts, and how social interactions at the gym often take place in a non-verbal dimension (cf. Collins 2010; Skinner 2010). This extract also underscores the importance of the physicality of the body in the transmission of non-verbal information at Kwaan-saa-maat Gym.

There is also a need to problematise what one observes in the field. Williams (1999) argues that ocularcentrism, the epistemological privileging of the visual over the other senses, is influenced by Western schools of thought and has resulted in perceiving bodily positions over movement. The ramification of this reductionistic perception is that in many publications "a series of photographs, sketches, diagrams, or positions of limbs plotted on a two-dimensional graph are presented as records of movement" (Farnell 1994, 929). In actual fact, this often fails to convey much sense of what the performer actually looks, sounds, or feels like. Performance ethnography provides the conceptual space for affective elements and the dynamic flow of actions over positions. One way to translate theory into praxis would have been the utilisation of video clips in my academic research. Video clips might be able to better capture the sensorial elements at the gym, the constant flow of bodies over physical and social space. However, for the purpose of this academic research, I attempted to write in an embodied style of writing that pays attention to the lived experiences of my participants.

A methodology that intimately situates me in the lives of my participants, that entails my living on the same premises as my participants, also raises an ethical conundrum. Although the individuals at the gym are aware of my dual identities as a researcher and a martial artist, their constant oscillation between being an informant, participant, and friend necessitates the reflexive question of what constitutes usable data. Another concern is that if I constantly remind them of my status as a researcher, not only will I disrupt the ongoing social drama and break the conversational flow but I may also create a rather contrived atmosphere as individuals restrain their thoughts and deeds (Ellis 1986). Interestingly, most of the participants at the gym demonstrated a high level of reflexivity and awareness about my presence at the gym, at times questioning me about the progress of my research, asking how many interviews I had conducted, whether can I send them the finished product, and even jokingly telling me to omit certain sexual innuendos and derogatory comments they had made. Jack, for example, exemplifies the level of self-reflexivity displayed by some of the participants at the gym:

> Do you want a tip Lionel? For your writing, you should write about all the kicking and clinching. That is what Muay Thai is! How are the interviews coming along? You should interview yourself! Ask yourself the same questions you've been asking everyone! It will be interesting! You should do it soon.

At another level, this vignette also reflects the continuous negotiation between my participants and myself as a researcher. Jack recognises certain actions as data and is not inviting but exhorting me to enact my status as a researcher. These incidents forced me to be more critical and self-aware of my conduct while I am out in the field.

Throughout the text, I elect to use the term "participant" instead of "informant," despite the latter term being traditionally used by anthropologists. This is because individuals chose, on their own accord, to participate in the various facets of life at the gym. The term "participant" also highlights the collaborative nature of the activities undertaken and collapses the hierarchical boundaries of power that the term "informant" connotes. This corresponds to Tillmann-Healy's (2003, 745) advice of "treat[ing] participants with an ethic of friendship. We can solicit fears and concerns, listen closely and respond compassionately, and use such exchanges to refine the study and direct its implications" as a way to avoid objectifying or manipulating one's participants. This framework that is based upon friendship further delineates the importance of reciprocity, equity, and self-reflexivity (Seidman 1998). By blurring the dichotomy between researcher and researched, such a framework helps to assuage certain ethical fears of exploitation and manipulation that I may have. I do acknowledge that not all friendships formed are valued equally but I hoped that by attempting to treat every participant as a friend, it may ameliorate possible objectification of the participants.

Despite being acutely aware of the subjective nature of one's memory, expediencies in the field necessitates that field notes can only be jotted down either at the end of the training session or at the end of the day. Whenever possible, brief notes were typed out on my iPhone to jolt my memory. Given that the participants often use their electronic devices such as a notebook or iPhone to access the Internet even during mealtimes, my frequent use of my iPhone did not attract any undue attention. Guys use the Internet for various reasons such as keeping in contact with their family and friends, whiling away the minutes, or even hooking up with the local women.

SEMI-STRUCTURED IN-DEPTH INTERVIEWS

In addition, qualitative interviews were conducted with 18 participants to uncover the "webs of significance" (Geertz 2001, 261) about the social reality of the gym and to "develop a level of detail about the participants and be highly involved in the actual experiences of the participants" (Creswell 2003, 181). The discrepancy between the number of interviews conducted and the number of people I knew at the gym throughout the duration of my entire stay is due largely to time constrains. Exacerbated by the gym's transient social environment as participants come and go, there was simply not enough time to establish rapport with some of the participants. After departing from the field site, I still maintain contact with the participants, occasionally continuing our friendly tête-à-tête over the Internet and if need be, follow-up on particular themes or queries.

Complementing the use of performance ethnography, interviews, which calls for my participants to be self-reflexive, allow for a more nuanced understanding of their motivations behind their taking up martial arts. The constant adjustments to my research schedule reflect the dynamic nature of social reality as emergent themes develop during my time out in the field. Importantly, these in-depth interviews function as a safeguard against any normative assumptions I may have about the ongoing social interaction occurring at the gym (Seale 1998) and were a vital means of getting deeper insights into what I was learning.

Prior to the interview, I obtained my participants' informed consent and agreement to record the interviews. The recordings and transcripts are kept under lock and key. To ensure the anonymity of the participants, pseudonyms are used throughout the text. The interviews were conducted at the premises of the gym either after training sessions or after meals. At times, interviews were conducted in front of the other guys as the participant did not perceive the need for privacy or given the public nature of the gym, some guys chancing upon the interview may decide to stay and listen, voicing their comments only after the interview was done. While not totally welcomed, these "intrusions" can be seen as informal focus groups, which help to furbish data that arises out of the group's synergy (Morgan 1988) and allows for greater spontaneity amongst informants (Stewart et al. 2007). In addition, in order to "naturalise" my presence at the gym, to demonstrate the overt nature of my research and as a martial artist attempting to integrate himself into this social environment, it would be awkward to consciously object to the presence of others, who had already been interviewed themselves, when they "intrude."

In addition, photographs depicting participants either in training or engaging in leisure activities after training are another source of data. These photographs convey the kind of body imagery the guys wish to portray to the world and the techniques of the body (Mauss 1973) that they come to internalise through their martial arts training. I am under no illusion that this ethnographic evidence can be presented as objective facts given how it is:

> first created in the field. They are created anew whenever the fieldworker, back home, re-examines fieldnotes and is transported back into the field experience. And they are created yet again when fieldworkers discuss their experiences with other anthropologists (Schultz and Lavenda 1990, 69).

However, these photographs constitute important data and are also a means by which to jog my memory.

EMBODIMENT, REPRESENTATION, AND WRITING

This book is about embodied experience, and the centrality of the body in somatic cultures. Toren's (2009, 136) enjoinment to "as clearly as I can, describe how humans constitute themselves as unique beings who can nevertheless be seen to be the always dynamic product of the history of intersubjective relations in whose terms they live their lives" is an important one. The politics of representation is a pertinent and recurrent one that particularly plagues performance studies and studies relating to the body and the senses. The main issues are how one does justice to the somatic movement and experiences being studied and whether in translating these experiences through the medium of language for an academic audience, the meaning or essence would be lost or distorted. Verisimilitude, the attempt to capture some semblance of the lived reality of my informants, remains central in these studies.

For this research, I deliberately chose to write in a style that incorporates the personal experiences and emotions of both researcher and researched. This embodied style of writing is reflective of a shift in previous ethnographic works. Previously, academics were often enjoined to write in an "objective" manner that silences the voice of the subject in favour of the researcher's authoritarian voice. The "crisis of representation" that swept through ethnographic writing from the mid-1980s, after the publication of Clifford and Marcus's edited volume *Writing Culture* (1986), is summarised by Conquergood (1991) as the tension between an embodied style of writing vis-à-vis a style of writing that is perceived to be objective and rational. There is thus the need to move beyond presenting data as a "detached observer using neutral language" to incorporating the lived and embodied experience of the researcher in the writing process (Conquergood 1991, 179). A germane point, to paraphrase Gouldner (1974, 10), is that objectivity is not attained through protocols that mechanically ensure the neutrality of social facts but via critical self-awareness; the ability to confront one's positionality, interests, and desires; and the ramifications these have on one's ontology and epistemology. Situating this academic research within a self-reflexive paradigm that calls for researchers to construe research not as a value-free scientific inquiry (Cook and Fonow 1986; Rapport 2010; Reinharz 1992) but as an interactive relationship situated in a context permeated by dimensions of class, power, emotionality, and intersubjectivity (Holstein and Gubrium 1995) further supports the need to move beyond objective and disembodied styles of representation. These theoretical underpinnings sensitise me to the politics of representation and raise the difficult questions of (1) how can the transmission of embodied knowledge across bodies be put into words? and (2) how can verisimilitude be conveyed through my vignettes of participants?

Extracts from my field notes are one mechanism by which I can convey my personal embodied experiences as my corporeal self became reconfigured through learning Muay Thai. Secondly, they can help to convey something of the atmosphere at the gym. My field notes and transcripts were subjected to open coding and thematic analysis (Manson 2002), as categories of analysis are shaped by the emergent data and the patterns of reality that emerge (Charmaz 2002; Lofland and Lofland 1995).

In this chapter, I have discussed the various ways in which the sensorial and bodily sensations experienced by the men can be comprehended and translated for the benefit of an academic audience. In the following chapters, I will further expound on how this somatic culture manifests itself in the everyday lived realities of the gym and becomes intertwined with notions of identity formation.

References

Buckland, T. J. (1999). [Re]Constructing meanings: The dance ethnographer as keeper of the truth. In T. J. Buckland (Ed.), *Dance in the field. Theory, methods and issues in dance ethnography*. Great Britain: Macmillan Press Ltd.

Charmaz, K. (2002). Qualitative interviewing and grounded theory analysis. In J. F. Gubrium & J. A. Holstein (Eds.), *Handbook of interview research context and method*. Thousand Oaks, CA: Sage.

Clifford, J., & Marcus, G. E. (Eds.). (1986). *Writing culture: The poetics and politics of ethnography: A school of American research advanced seminar*. Berkeley: University of California Press.

Collins, P. (2010). The ethnographic self as resource? In P. Collins & A. Gallinat (Eds.), *The ethnographic self as resource. Writing memory and experience into ethnography*. New York: Berghahn Books.

Conquergood, D. (1991). Rethinking ethnography: Towards a critical cultural politics. *Communication Monographs, 58*(1), 179–194.

Cook, J. A., & Fonow, M. M. (1986). Knowledge and women's interest: Issues of epistemology and methodology in feminist sociological research. *Sociological Inquiry, 56*(1), 2–27.

Creswell, J. W. (2003). *Research design: Qualitative, quantitative, and mixed methods approaches*. Thousand Oaks, CA: Sage Publications Inc.

Denzin, N. K. (2003). *Performance ethnography: Critical pedagogy and the politics of culture*. Thousand Oaks, CA: Sage.

Dickson-Swift, V., James, E. L., Kippen, S., & Liamputtong, P. (2009). Researching sensitive topics qualitative research as emotion work. *Qualitative Research, 9*(1), 61–79.

Ellis, C. (1986). *Fisher folk: Two communities on Chesapeake Bay*. Kentucky: University Press of Kentucky.

Farnell, B. (1994). Ethno-graphics and the moving body. *Journal of the Royal Anthropological Institute, 29*(4), 929–974.

Geertz, C. (2001)[1973]. Thick description: Toward an interpretive theory of culture. In N. K. Denzin, & Y. S. Lincoln (Eds.), *The American tradition in qualitative research*. Thousand Oaks: Sage.

Giddens, A. (1984). *The constitution of society: Outline of the theory of structuration*. Berkeley: University of California Press.

Goffman, E. (1971). *The presentation of self in everyday life*. Harmondsworth: Penguin.

Gore, G. (1999). Textual fields: Representations in dance ethnography. In T. J. Buckland (Ed.), *Dance in the field. Theory, methods and issues in dance ethnography*. Great Britain: Macmillan Press Ltd.

Gouldner, A. (1974). *The dark side of the dialectic: Towards a new objectivity*. Dublin: The Economic and Research Institute.

Grau, A. (1999). Fieldwork, politics and power. In T. J. Buckland (Ed.), *Dance in the field. Theory, methods and issues in dance ethnography*. Great Britain: Macmillan Press Ltd.

Green, K. (2011). It hurts so it is real: Sensing the seduction of mixed martial arts. *Social and Cultural Geography, 12*(4), 377–396.

Gubrium, J. F., & Holstein, J. A. (2000). Analysing interpretive practice. In N. K. Denzin & Y. S. Lincoln (Eds.), *Handbook of qualitative research* (2nd ed.). London: Sage Publications Inc.

Holstein, J. A., & Gubrium, J. F. (1995). *The active interview*. Thousand Oaks, CA: Sage.

Howes, D. (2003). *Sensual relations: Engaging the senses in culture and social theory*. Ann Arbor, MI: University of Michigan Press.

Howes, D. (2004a). *Sport, professionalism and pain*. London: Routledge.

Howes, D. (Ed.). (2004b). *Empire of the senses: The sensual culture reader*. Oxford and New York: Berg.

Kaeppler Adrienne, L. (1999). The mystique of fieldwork. In T. J. Buckland (Ed.), *Dance in the field. Theory, methods and issues in dance ethnography*. Great Britain: Macmillan Press Ltd.

Kershaw, B., Miller, L./Whalley, J., & Lee, R./Pollard, N. (2011). Practice as research: Transdisciplinary innovation in action. In: B. Kershaw & H. Nicholson (Eds.), *Research methods in theatre and performance*. Edinburgh: Edinburgh University Press.

Leigh Foster, S. (2003). The Ballerina's Phallic Pointe. In A. Jones (Ed.), *The feminism and visual cultural reader*. London and New York: Routledge.

Lofland, J., & Lofland, L. (1995). *Analysing social settings: A guide to qualitative observation and analysis*. Belmont, CA: Wadsworth Publishing Co.

Manson, J. (2002). *Qualitative researching* (2nd ed.). Great Britain: MPG Books Group.

Massumi, B. (2002). *Parables for the virtual movement, affect, sensation*. Durham, NC: Duke University Press.

Mauss, M. (1973). Techniques of the body. *Economy and Society, 2*(1), 70–88.

Morgan, D. L. (1988). *Focus groups as qualitative research.* Thousand Oaks, CA: Sage.

Okley, J. (2007). Fieldwork embodied. In C. Shilling (Ed.), *Embodying sociology: Retrospect, progress and prospects.* Malden, MA: Blackwell.

Parker-Starbuck, J., & Mock, R. (2011). Researching the body in/as performance. In B. Kershaw & H. Nicholson (Eds.), *Research methods in theatre and performance.* Edinburgh: Edinburgh University Press.

Polanyi, M. (1983). *The tacit dimension.* Garden City, New York: Doubleday and Company.

Potter, C. (2008). Sense of motion, senses of self: Becoming a dancer. *Ethnos, 73*(4), 444–465.

Rapport, N. (2010). The ethics of participant observation: Personal reflections on fieldwork in England. In P. Collins & A. Gallinat (Eds.), *The ethnographic self as resource. Writing memory and experience into ethnography.* New York: Berghahn Books.

Reinharz, S. (1992). *Feminist methods in social research.* New York: Oxford University Press.

Samudra, J. K. (2008). Memory in our body: Thick participation and the translation of kinesthetic experience. *American Ethnologist, 35*(4), 665–681.

Schatzki, T. R., Knorr Cetina, K., & von Savigny, E. (Eds.). (2000). *The practice turn in contemporary theory.* Edinburgh: Edinburgh University Press.

Schultz, E., & Lavenda, R. (1990). *Cultural anthropology: A perspective on the human condition.* St Paul, MN: West Publishing Company.

Seale, C. (1998). *Researching society and culture.* London: Sage.

Seidman, I. (1998). *Interviewing as qualitative research. A guide for researchers in education and the social sciences* (2nd ed.). New York: Teachers College Press.

Seymour, W. (2007). Exhuming the body: Revisiting the role of the visible body in ethnographic research. *Qualitative Health Resource, 17*(9), 1188–1197.

Skinner, J. (2010). Leading questions and body memories: A case of phenomenology and physical ethnography in the dance interview. In P. Collins & A. Gallinat (Eds.), *The ethnographic self as resource. Writing memory and experience into ethnography.* New York: Berghahn Books.

Stewart, D. W., Shamdasani, P. N., & Rook, D. W. (2007). *Focus groups. Theory and practices* (2nd ed.). United States of America: Sage.

Tedlock, B. (2000). Ethnography and ethnographic representation. In N. K. Denzin & Y. S. Lincoln (Eds.), *Handbook of qualitative research* (2nd ed.). London: Sage.

Tillmann-Healy, L. M. (2003). Friendship as method. *Qualitative Inquiry, 9,* 729–749.

Toren, C. (2009). Intersubjectivity as epistemology. *Social Analysis, 53*(2), 130–146.

Turner, V. W. (1696). *The ritual process: Structure and anti-structure.* Chicago: Aldine.

Wacquant, L. (2004). *Body and soul, notebooks of an apprentice boxer*. Oxford: Oxford University Press.

Wacquant, L. (2009). Habitus as topic and tool: Reflections on becoming a Prizefighter. In W. Shaffir, A. Puddephatt, & S. Kleinknecht (Eds.), *Ethnographies revisited*. New York: Routledge.

Williams, D. (1999). Fieldwork. In T. J. Buckland (Ed.), *Dance in the field. Theory, methods and issues in dance ethnography*. Great Britain: Macmillan Press Ltd.

CHAPTER 3

The Lived Realities at the Gym

Abstract In this chapter, I attempt to portray the ethnographic reality of the MMA gym by describing the gym's physical layout and a typical day in the life of a fighter. Vis-à-vis the vignettes and individuals' experiences at the gym and the topics that were frequently articulated during moments of leisure, I demonstrate how the gym exists as a liminal space that stands apart from the everyday life of the participants due to its isolated location as well as to the social norms and regulations that promote an almost exclusively masculine ethos.

In this chapter, I attempt to portray the ethnographic reality of the MMA gym by describing the gym's physical layout and a typical day in the life of a fighter. Vis-à-vis the vignettes and individuals' experiences at the gym and the topics that were frequently articulated during moments of leisure, I argue that bodily experiences and sensations are central to this somatic culture and the pervasive masculine ethos that exists there. By exploring the nuances between what is often expressed by the participants and the contradictions that occur in the everyday interactions at the gym, I will illustrate how a particular image is maintained of the gym as a place of strict and harsh regimes and of the men's identities as tough, devoted fighters. I shall argue here that the gym is a liminal space and that liminality within this somatic culture is not simply the result of structural changes/dissonances but embodied experiences as well. I suggest the use of the term *embodied liminality* as a way to further comprehend this

© The Editor(s) (if applicable) and The Author(s) 2016
Loh H.L.L, *The Body and Senses in Martial Culture*,
DOI 10.1057/978-1-137-55742-1_3

phenomenon. Liminality refers to a marginal state, a state whereby the individual is in a "kind of suspended animation," divorced from the everyday mores of society (Leach 1967, 134). I will later expound upon how this liminal state is both created and experienced through the everyday lives of the gym and the centrality of the body in connecting these diverse threads of the men's lives.

THE DAILY ROUTINES OF A FIGHTER

This is an account of the bodily regimes available to participants at the gym. There are two training sessions in a day, and training takes place 6 days a week with Sunday being the designated rest day. At about 6.30 a.m., the clanging of the bells will serve as a wake-up call to the men, and at 7 a.m., training commences with an 8.5 km run around the lake. After the run, there is a short skipping session of approximately 20 min before one puts on the hand wraps and shadow boxes for five rounds. Each round lasts for about 5 min, and at the end of each round, one is to do 20 sit-ups/push-ups. Following this is another four to five rounds of padwork with the Thai trainers before one practises his punches and kicks on the bags. Padwork refers to a fighter with his hands wrapped up and wearing gloves, punching and kicking the pads held by another trainer/fighter, while kicking and punching the bags is also known as bagwork. Two hundred kicks, 100 knees, and 200 sit-ups then mark the end of the morning training. Knees, where one uses the knee as the striking point of contact, is a unique feature of Muay Thai.

At approximately 9.30 a.m., breakfast is served. Meals at the gym follow a typical menu of rice, meat and vegetable dishes, soup, and fresh fruit. After breakfast, the men either adjourn back to their rooms for a much-needed rest or head down to town. As lunch is not included in the training and accommodation package offered, the men either go to town on their rental motorbikes or purchase their meals from the gym's kitchen. At about 3.30 p.m., the bell rings again, signalling the start of the next training session. Due to the heat of the afternoon sun, the men often go for a shorter run. Similar to the morning routine, once the men are back from the run, they skip and shadow box before engaging in either sparring or padwork. Mondays and Fridays are for Muay Thai sparring, allowing one to hone one's punches and kicks. Wednesdays are for boxing sparring, in which only punches are used. On Tuesdays,

Thursdays, and Saturdays, the men will take a break from sparring and concentrate on their techniques. This will take about 30–40 min. Once the men are done with the sparring or technical component, there is clinch training followed by a few rounds of bagwork. Clinching in Muay Thai entails being in extremely close proximity with one's opponent and delivering knees to the ribs and waiting for an opportunity to slam one's opponent to the ground. The training then ends with 200 kicks, 100 knees, and 200 sit-ups. For participants who are learning both Muay Thai and MMA, after the sparring or technical component, they would head over into the MMA ring and proceed to learn how to do takedowns, grapples, and locks for another hour. At about 6.30 p.m., dinner is served. After dinner, the men either idle around the gym or catch movies and watch telecast MMA fights together. More often than not, the men, at least those who know how to ride a motorbike and have rented one, together with a passenger, will head out to town for leisure activities such as grocery shopping, drinking, eating, clubbing, and massages.

This description of the life at the gym can be considered an ideal type. When a newcomer enquires about the training routines, the men will highlight how intense the training is, with fighters training six times a week, twice daily. In practice, I noticed that the participants do not adhere to this regime for various reasons such as recovering from injuries, having insomnia the night before, or just wanting a respite from the training. Ray, 19, a British undergraduate, has the opinion that it is actually not that ideal to subject the body to such continuous training:

> You immerse yourself in the training and focus. That is all you care about. But then unless you are a professional fighter, I don't think that is healthy. I don't think it is healthy for someone who is not a professional fighter to focus their whole life... focusing a part of their life solely on training. Because there are other elements of life and you lose the perspective to the bigger picture. There is more to life than training. You know I found myself almost getting depressed because all I did was train. I wake up in the morning, train, go back to sleep, wake up... be sitting there for 3 hours thinking to myself what am I going to do you know? I got nothing... Waiting for training and training again and then having the same problem [of finding activities to engage oneself outside of training] at night. You need more stimulation than that. Particularly if you are an intellectual person that needs to be stimulated.

This disjuncture between the "ideal" training schedule at the gym and reality reveals that the "ideal" is something of a fiction that the men actively maintain to newcomers. This fiction masks the various reasons why the men do not train as regularly as the schedule dictates and helps to sustain their identity as masculine, devoted fighters. Goffman's (1971) concept of dramaturgy illustrates how the enactment of a particular front to social others is achieved through the performativity of the body. Performance, defined as "the activity of an individual which occurs during a period marked by his continuous presence before a particular set of observers and which has some influence on the observers" (Goffman 1971, 22), is intertwined with the cultural attribution of social messages to bodily expressions and display and one's own sense of identity (1971, 36). Parallels can be drawn to this phenomenon at the gym where the "front" and "back" stages refer to the physical regimes scheduled at the gym versus what actually happens in practice, respectively. The fiction at the gym, which can be partially attributed to the desires of the men to express their identity as masculine fighters, is then responsible for this cleavage between the "front" and "back" stages.

In his previous visit to the gym about a year ago, Aaron remarked on how the trainers used to bang on the fighters' doors every morning to get ready for the morning training. This practice has since lapsed but individuals are still willing to pay for what they consider to be a monastic lifestyle, albeit without the harsh regimentations. This fiction, constitutive of the larger gym culture, will be further elaborated in the subsequent sections.

DESCRIPTION OF THE GYM

A brief description of the premises of the gym will serve to highlight not only how their passion for martial arts unites individuals from diverse backgrounds but also how the living and training spaces at the gym conspire to make communal life there unavoidable. The gym is a "short-lived society" (Foster 1986) in that limited time and a structured training schedule intensifies these societal interactions. Kwaan-saa-maat Gym is located about 15 minutes' ride away from the town centre, and aside from a couple of restaurants and grocery stores, there is little in the way of entertainment. Unless one knows how to ride a motorbike and rents one from the gym, it is hard to partake of Ubon's nightlife or get to know people outside the gym. There is also a language barrier that needs to be traversed. Mobility or the lack thereof becomes an important factor in shaping communal life at the gym as most individuals often spent their time either resting within the privacy of their rooms or talking with the other men at particular sites at the gym.

Kwaan-saa-maat Gym is made up of two adjacent two-storey buildings that are separated by a small road. The main building consists of the kitchen, a shop selling Muay Thai and MMA equipment, a laundry room, and rooms for accommodation. In front of the kitchen are two stone tables and benches, which are mainly used by the Thai staff during their mealtimes. Individuals who occasionally buy their lunch from the kitchen may gather here to bond over lunch. The other building houses the gym facilities and more rooms. Despite being Spartan in its furnishings, each twin-sharing room comes with an en suite bathroom. A sign saying "Kwaan-saa-maat Gym," written in Thai script, marks the entrance of the gym. There are two boxing rings, one of which is located just outside the gym. Surrounding the perimeter of the boxing ring inside the gym are boxing gloves, pads, and hand wraps. In front of this ring are three stone tables and benches where the men gather to take their meals and chat. The concrete floor of the gym is covered with foam mats, and beside this boxing ring are six punching bags. As one walks further into the gym, to the left there is an area equipped with weights and barbells for weightlifting. Further in, situated near the rooms is an octagonal MMA cage where MMA lessons are conducted.

Aside from the stone benches, there are few alternative spaces for social interaction where the men can debate the finer points of martial arts, the lifestyle in Thailand or topics such as food, women, and sex. Being MMA aficionados, most individuals are able to reel off the names of various professional fighters and engage in detailed discussions of landmark professional fights. However, the men value their privacy and seldom invite others into the personal spaces of their rooms. These communal places are thus the locales in which the masculine ethos and the somatic culture of the gym are shaped. As sites of sociability, failure to partake in the ongoing social interactions there is frowned upon. For example, when Peder failed to appear for training and communal meals for 3 days in a row due to a fight that sprang from a disagreement, electing to stay in his room, he became the butt of jokes. The men were quick to comment how Peder was "sulking in his room like a child" and were scornful of how he did not turn up regularly for training.

THE SOMATIC AND MASCULINE GYM CULTURE

In this section, I illustrate the somatic and masculine gym culture as gleaned from the conversations between the men. This somatic element is imbued in topics that range across dietary intake, training regimes, sports, and martial arts. Previous work done on somatic cultures such as rugby, windsurfing, skydiving, and endurance racing (Celsi et al. 1993; Ewert 1994; Kay and Laberge 2002a, b; Wheaton 2000) highlights how within these social worlds there exist "unique sets of special norms, values, beliefs, styles, moral principles, performance standards and similar shared representations"(Stebbins 1999, 71). Mills (1940, 904) theorises how linguistic behaviour has a "social function of coordinating diverse actions" and that individuals "discern situations with particular vocabularies, and it is in terms of some delimited vocabulary that they anticipate consequences of conduct. Stable vocabularies of motives link anticipated consequences and specific actions" (1940, 906). Conversations carried out at the abovementioned sites of sociality are never simply about personal gripes or hobbies but also reflective of the larger social milieu that the men have chosen to embed themselves in and the identities which they wish to portray and perform. In the course of their everyday conversations, most participants demonstrate an in-depth awareness of not just their own bodies but other bodies as well. This is illustrated when Karl nonchalantly discussed how much weight the various fighters at the gym need to gain or lose in order to be in an advantageous weight category. For topics such as MMA and sports, the men often discuss the merits of having particular kinds of bodies that certain activities demand of them. In their discussion of rugby, the men talked about how the New Zealand All Blacks were renowned not only for their prowess on the field but also for their huge physiques. There appeared to be for the men a correlation between different phenotypes pertaining to bodily sizes and nationalities/race. When Jack, who has a rather lanky frame, mentioned how although the sport was interesting, he was too small, Vernon was quick to reply, "You can come and play in Singapore!"

In addition to portraying their bodily knowledge through their discussion with others, through their everyday lives, the men also actively attempt to shape and discipline their bodies. The men actively try to control their weight and discipline their bodies through stratagems such as dietary intake, the use of supplements, and physical activities. These activities, informed by scientific discourses, range from restricting their carbohydrate intake to even contemplating the use of steroids or growth hormones. This minute devotion to one's activities that is governed by scientific discourses parallels the fanaticism exhibited by participants in other somatic cultures such as gym-goers (Brown and Graham 2008; Crossley 2006; Johansson 1996; Rantala and Lehtonen 2001; Reid 1994). This comment, occurring at the dinner table, typifies this relentless disciplining of their bodies:

> Kelvin, 28, South African, schoolteacher: I don't think I should eat a lot of food for breakfast today since I didn't manage to wake up in the morning to train...

Kelvin's comment, contextualised within the larger masculine environment of the gym, is an attempt to perform one's masculinity and identity as a disciplined fighter. Bourdieu's (1977, 1984, 1990a, b, 1998) concepts of "field," "habitus," and "capital" provides a framework by which to understand the vocabulary of motivations and actions employed by the men at the gym. Within a particular field, different participants have different levels of involvement depending on what their stakes and interest are. As a theoretical tool by which to understand the practices and interactions of a particular group, participants in a "field" often vie for "capital" to demonstrate their allegiance and competence to social others. These comments constitute one aspect of bodily capital, an idiosyncratic form of capital that has particular value within the field of the gym itself. Bodily capital, as a form of cultural capital, refers to possessing knowledge of pugilistic information such as the weight categories of various fighters and (as Wacquant noted of boxers in France) the "diffuse complex of postures and (physical and mental) gestures that, being continually (re)produced in and through the very functioning of the gym, exist in a sense only in action, and in the traces that this action leaves within (and upon) bodies" (Wacquant 2004, 59). Performing the identity of a disciplined fighter entails involving the body in particular figurations of physical regimes that include eschewing particular kinds of food and restricting one's diet. Paul is an American professional fighter, aged 34. His comment epitomised this discourse of constant sacrifice and abstinence:

> But you know like anything, you want to be a CEO of a company, you want to rise to the top, you better want to sacrifice. If you don't want to sacrifice, be satisfied to sell cigarettes at 7-11. The more you want to achieve

anything, the price of sacrifice is greater. That's why it frustrates me that so many people in high school say stuff like I could have been a good fighter. I said well ya, maybe, you know, but the problem is you like to eat pizza. You don't like to sacrifice.

This is seen as an accepted norm amongst fighters. Venkat, 25, an Indian professional fighter, also talks about how prior to every weigh-in, he dehydrates his body by staying in the sauna and abstaining from food and drink.

Yet food is also a paradoxical source of pleasure. The men frequent Swensens, an ice-cream parlour in town, at least once a week to reward themselves for devoting the week to training. Simultaneously, they are aware that such indulgences come at a price. Karl puts it thus:

> I put on weight to about 61 kg on Sundays [from all the feasting at Swensens and other restaurants] and then I have to run to be back to my original 57 kg. Sundays are the day you really enjoy yourself and then the next day it is so hard, cause you need to wake up for training again.

The men constantly oscillate between perceiving food as a pleasurable indulgence and deconstructing it as necessary and functional carbohydrates, proteins, and fats, and sanctions are applied on those who fail to exercise dietary discipline. When Peder failed to train one afternoon and announced that he had gorged on a huge burger, garlic bread, pancakes, and a fruit shake, the men met this revelation with silence, amazement, and scorn. Food and body image are closely linked, and the failure to regulate one's dietary intake symbolises an individual who gives into excesses, an individual who lacks willpower (Bruch 1997; Parasecoli 2005). Conversely, Kong, one of the Thai trainers, who is renowned for his love of whisky, is highly respected because as Karl comments, "Kong drinks like a fish but he can still fuck you up!" Individuals who do not subject their bodies to regulation and discipline and yet are still able to "fuck someone up" (i.e., fight effectively) are often talked about in admiring tones. This awe stems from the individual being a successful fighter despite ignoring the conventions of discipline and hard work. By treating fighters such as Kong, who does not adhere to a disciplined lifestyle, as exceptions to the rule, the men reaffirm to themselves the essence of what a good fighter should be. This simultaneously reaffirms the participants' commitment to a communal social order. Displaying admiration for non-conformist but successful fighters and marginalising fighters whose lacklustre career and abilities are the result of an undisciplined lifestyle is a mechanism by which essentialised ideas about the ideal fighter are perpetuated and propagated. By defining fighters such as Kong as out of the ordinary, the classification system of what a fighter should be remains intact, validating the sacrifices to which the men subject themselves.

This nuanced understanding of their bodies is something actively encouraged as it is fundamental to being a good fighter. A fighter who has mastery over his body will know the physiological limits of his own body, and this will help to prevent accidental injuries.

Vernon	I don't think I can train again today man... My shoulders are hurting and everything...
James	You should let the trainers know about it. So you can train and don't do particular exercises. You need to know your own body well. Like for me it hurts so I don't do hooks and elbows. You need to tell the trainers!

Through these vignettes of my participants and the everyday activities, I illustrate how disciplining of the body is not only part of everyday life at the gym, indeed it is one of the fundamental goals which some individuals seek. We can see, too, how the physical body is not only disciplined by the individual but also surveyed by other social actors. Whether the men are conscious of it or not, the minute detail and knowledge that they display about their own bodies and that of other social actors is atypical of most individuals. This knowledge is gleaned by conditioning the body through the rigours of training and careful observation of how bodies should move in combat.

At another level, demonstrating their bodily knowledge and the kind of bodily capital they possess is related to performing and reinforcing their identity as heterosexual, masculine males. A hypermasculine culture, where masculinity is put onto a pedestal, is endemic to most contact sports, in which characteristics of domination and physical aggression are valued (Burstyn 1999; Coakley 2001; Connell 1995; Crosset 1999; Messner 1990, 1992; Sabo 1994; Young et al. 1994). Contact sports are sites around which males construct hegemonic masculine identities (Kreager 2007). In a predominantly male environment, where bodily contact is frequent, given the physical nature of martial arts, the fear of each potentially homoerotic encounter needs to be actively repudiated (Bierly

1985; Heaven and Oxman 1999; Herek 2000; Kite 1984; Morrison et al. 1999; Sakalli 2002). Given the homosocial undercurrent in any sport that involves bodily contact, the onus is often upon newcomers to demonstrate their sexuality. For example, in Muir and Seitz's (2004) study of American collegiate rugby, they argue that the derogation of women and homosexuals becomes a mechanism by which to maintain and sustain hegemonic masculinity. Karl's seemingly random comment is reflective of the larger masculine ethos at the gym:

> You know how when you are in, say, Sweden? You see a tall blond chick and you go: 'She is hot!' But here in Thailand, you see a tall gorgeous chick you will go: 'Wait a minute is she a lady boy!' [laughs]

"Lady boy" is a derogatory term used in Thailand to describe transvestites. Similarly, when Venkrat first came to the gym, aside from talking about his training and dietary regimes, he also took pains to emphasise his heterosexuality to strangers:

> When I was in Bangkok, I hitched a ride with two ladies. It was only when they suggested that we should go to a hotel then I realised that they were lady boys! Man you can never tell in Thailand! [laughs] And there was another time when I was in Las Vegas, this guy was asking me for directions to a restaurant and after I accepted his offer to have a cup of coffee with me, he started to talk shit... fuck man... fucking homos!

These two vignettes demonstrate how heteronormativity can never even be taken for granted in a masculine environment. By vocalising their distaste for homosexuals and the lady boys, the men constantly deviantise these individuals as pollutive elements. Douglas (1966, 48) points out the underlying reasons behind such codifications:

> In short, our pollution behaviour is the reaction which condemns any object or idea likely to confuse or contradict cherished classifications.

Homophobia, which simultaneously rejects effeminacy and endorses masculinity (Thompson et al. 1985), maintains the boundaries between sexual and social relations in a homosocially stratified society (Britton 1990; Davies 1982; Greenberg and Bystyrn 1982; Morin and Garfinkle 1978) and is a cornerstone for identity formation. Identity formation, arising from the contention of "intersecting discourses" (Hall 1996), is an end-less process in which experiences continue to shape and structure one's subjectivity (Craib 1998). Although the crux of identity in modernity as postulated by Giddens (1991) is its reflexivity, one must accede that identity is about differences in that it is partly constructed in relation to the external other. As Hall (1996, 345) eloquently states:

> There is no identity that is without the dialogic relationship to the Other. The Other is not outside, but also inside the Self, the identity. So identity is a process, identity is split. Identity is not a fixed point but an ambivalent point. Identity is also the relationship of the Other to oneself.

Thailand's ambiguous sexual categories, as perceived by these heteronormative individuals, contest the normative boundaries of sexuality and sex and become the mirror by which the men formulate their sense of masculinity and identity as fighters. The gym's culture of heightened masculinity and discipline clashes with the Western, orientalistic discursive traditions that construct Thailand simultaneously as a haven of unbridled sexuality and a site of peril because of lady boys and homosexuals (Bishop and Robinson 1999; Cook and Jackson 1999; Jackson 1999; Jackson and Sullivan 1999; Storer 1999). Talking disparagingly about these sexual categories becomes a strategy adopted by the men to assert their masculinity. Butler (1990, 140) elucidated how gender as the "stylised repetition of acts" is crystallised through performative acts. Through these repetitive acts, whereby "the essence or identity that they otherwise purport to express are fabrications manufactured and sustained through corporeal signs and other discursive means" (Butler 1990, 136), secular knowledge regarding gender and social norms comes to have a hegemonic quality to the extent that social actors "come to believe and perform the mode of belief" (Butler 1990, 141). The need to constantly vocalise such sentiments in their everyday lives points to how the edifice of heteronormativity needs to be constantly performed and reiterated for its hegemony to be sustained.

The masculine environment at the gym resonates with Sanday's (1990) description of the fraternity subculture. In her work, *Fraternity Gang Rape*, Sanday argues that amongst male college students, there exist heteronormative and patriarchal social norms. These norms, sustained by the institutional arrangements of fraternities and the "social ideology of male dominance" (1990, 11), result in the men denigrating and objectifying women. Parallels can be made to the gym, a site where male fighters train in isolation from the rest of the world. This discourse is reflected through the everyday conversations where the men talk about women as being either prostitutes or sex objects. In addition, this denigration of women and talking about women in a derogatory manner not only occurs at the discursive level but also in the daily relations that the men have with the local Thai women. Given the relative isolation of the gym from the town and their unfamiliarity with Ubon, it is common for some of the men to get the local women who have their own means of transport, to pick them up for drinks and other amorous activities. These encounters, in which males construct Thai women as being docile and subservient, take on a racialised and gendered dimension (cf. Gilman 2002; Robinson 1996). Such affairs take place off the premises of the gym, since the owner prohibits the fighters from bringing people to sleep over at the gym as it may disrupt the fighters' concentration. Yet, Aaron's moment of vacillation over whether he should bring a woman that he met at the pubs back to the gym for sex, and his final decision not to out of respect for the place, points to the asymmetrical relations between the sexes. The gym is a liminal space, constructed as a site from which women, except those employed by the gym in domestic roles, are barred. The gym is thus an exclusive space which women are prohibited from entering. Paradoxically, although women are the medium by which men express their masculinity and virility, they are simultaneously constructed as a potential source of danger and unbridled sexuality that can imperil the fighters' concentration and focus. The inability to exercise one's willpower, whether regarding women or diet, is to give in to one's base desires, something that is antithetical for a fighter who symbolises discipline and sacrifice.

Within the confines of the gym, masculinity is not only constructed upon the sexual prowess of men vis-à-vis women but also in relation to their ability as fighters who are able to withstand the rigours of training. Masculine physiques, an important currency of bodily capital, highlight how body projects (Shilling 1993) transform the physicality of the body through bodily disciplines. As a signifier, the body communicates to others one's identity and commitment as a fighter. Muscular, scarred, and battered bodies possess the ability to command, respect, and bestow upon the individual a degree of authoritativeness. The men often elevate fighters who sustain injuries and put them on a pedestal. Injuries acquired in the course of training become symbols of one's baptism of fire, are never openly boasted about but stand as a silent testimony to others of one's devotion to the art. Examples of these visible bodily signifiers include bruised skin and blood on one's knuckles and shins and swelling in one's knuckles or joints. These emblems, as forms of bodily capital, are reflective of the pain and hardship that the men never explicitly vocalise but which are always used as a point of reference by their peers. Kelvin, for example, remarks:

> It seems like everyone is injured today! Shoulder [points to Vernon, James and himself], knee [points to Jack], elbow [points to Karl] and ankle [points to me]
> Karl [interrupts]: Everyone except for Peder! He does not really train anyway!

Such injuries can be seen as evidence that they are paying their dues to martial arts (Wacquant 2004). Masculinity is thus intertwined with the currency of bodily capital and is indexed through not just one's physical body but the ability of the body to sustain, endure, and triumph in the face of adversity and pain.

These shared meanings of what the ideal martial arts body is may be partially informed by the men's own training experiences. Aside from becoming more focused and disciplined in their lives, many of the men talked about the results of their training that manifest in their bodies as faster reflexes, a leaner physique, and an increase in agility. Venkat, for example, actually apologised when he was unable to react fast enough to catch me when I slipped and fell:

> Sorry bro! It happened so fast and I could not catch you in time! I should have been able too... My reflexes should be faster than this...

An individual's physique is not only transformed by increasing levels of muscularity but also the callusing of particular points on the body, such as the elbows, shins, and knuckles, that are used to strike one's opponents. Spencer (2009, 140) invents the term *body callusing* to refer to the "complex and variable combinations of reflexive body techniques, hardening the fighter's body so that it can withstand the rigours of the sport." Intimately involved in the lived spaces of the gym, my body was inevitably transformed in the course of my fieldwork. Bruises marked my shins due to my constantly kicking the boxing bags, and comments were often made about how I would be a better fighter and would get tougher.

Michael	Your bruises are fucked man! Does it hurt?
L.L	Yeah but I guess I will get better from this. So does your shin still hurt from kicking the bags?
Michael	No man, not since the last time I was in Thailand, last November? I was in Phuket for 3 weeks. It hurts but after a week back in Norway it was okay. After that, I train again and it didn't hurt at all. You want to fuck people up? You got to experience the pain and harden your body!

Body callusing, which involves pain, allows the fighter to comprehend and thrive in this lived space. Body callusing necessitates a physical transformation in the fighter's body, and this is not only symbolic of one's status but also reflective of one's ability in the boxing ring. Carnal knowledge, through external stimulus, provides an avenue to clearly delineate the limits of the body and the need to acquire more bodily techniques. Carnal knowledge also functions as a feedback mechanism by which their bodies validate the men's training and boosts their confidence in themselves (Green 2011). This sense of masochism is also seen in my previous example of Ivar's stoicism with regard to the numerous bruises that decorated his entire shin. These bodily markers, constructed as masculine, are also a way by which one recognises a fellow martial artist on the street. David, 33, a Danish professional fighter, talks about how he is able to recognise a fighter:

| L.L | So what is the body type of a fighter? |
| David | It's hard to explain because sometimes, I see some guys that are really in shape but I can't really make out if they do cross-training or they are a fighter. But then when I can't make up my mind, I just look at the face and I can see. Obvious things as scars and rubber nose, flat cheekbones and cauliflower ears because they have been punched a lot. |

In *Techniques of the Body*, Mauss (2006, 83) expounds upon how "the body is man's first and most natural instrument…man's first and most natural technical object, and at the same time technical means, is his body" and that "techniques are thus human norms of training" (2006, 85). These techniques, the basis on which differentiations in somatic movement are created, allow discerning observers like David to recognise bodies that have been conditioned by martial disciplines. In Chap. 4, I will further elaborate upon the sensory dimensions of how individuals learn to embody martial practices.

Thus, we can conclude that due to the training and somatic culture within which the men have embedded their bodies, they possess a heightened sensitivity about their body and its possible limitations. Having a repository of intimate knowledge of the masculine body is a hallmark of a good fighter. Intertwined with performing the identity of a fighter are prevalent discourses regarding masculinity, heteronormativity, and masochism. Masculinity does not operate simply on the discursive level but is embodied through the narratives and actions of the men vis-à-vis women and transgressive categories such as homosexuals or lady boys. The gym's masculine ethos must in turn be contextualised in relation to the way in which the gym is constructed as a liminal space. This liminality derives not only from the fact that women are largely excluded from this male domain but also from its existence as a sphere that is separate from their mundane everyday lives back home. Within the gym, there thus exist multiple layers of inclusion and exclusion, comradeship, and alienation.

THE GYM: A LIMINAL SPACE

Except for time outside of training, where one is at liberty to engage in leisure activities, life at the gym appears to be highly structured and regimented. I argue that the liminality of the gym operates on two different dimensions. For foreigners, the lifestyle at the gym, where one is isolated from family and friends, and immerses oneself in a communitas of martial artists, poses a radical break from life back in their home countries. Andrew, 30, a Chinese professional fighter, summarises life at the gym as "a good life…hard training, eat, shower, sleep and train again. Every day passes fast." When asked what is the appeal of training at the gym, the men were quick to reply about how there are no distractions here as compared to the gyms at Phuket or Bangkok. This is summarised in Karl's comment:

> I wanted to get out of way from touristy place. There are just too many distractions with partying and people hustling you. There are many things to do and it is just more stressful you know. More traffic, more bars that people go to, girls, so many things to distract you, put you off your Muay Thai. Cheap alcohol, the beaches and stuff whereas out here there is less to do, enough to keep you entertained but you just train and that is what you do you know? Don't go do anything else except to train so it is good that way. I wanted to be out here where it's relaxed.

Situated away from possible distractions, the gym is symbolically and spatially constructed as an alternative, liminal universe. This resonates with Van Gennep's (1960, 3) analysis of human life as governed by periodicity with transitions and movements at the peripheries. Turner (1974, 232) acknowledges the intellectual debt to Van Gennep with regard to the concept of liminality:

> Liminality is a term borrowed from Arnold Van Gennep's formulation of rites de passage, 'transition rites'- which accompany every change of state or social position, or certain points in age. These are marked by three phrases: separation, margin (or *limen*-the Latin for threshold, signifying the great importance of real or symbolic thresholds at this middle period of the rites, though cunicular, 'being in a tunnel', would better describe the quality of this phase, in many cases, its hidden nature, its sometimes mysterious darkness), and reaggregation.

In *Liminality and Communitas*, Turner (2008, 327) defines liminal entities as being in a cultural miasma, "neither here nor there; they are betwixt and between the positions assigned and arrayed by law, custom, convention and ceremonial." Liminal or transgressive states assume a priori the existence of a boundary, an acknowledgement of that which should not be defied. Preceding what can be labelled as a transgressive act would be a recognition of a core. This core or "constitution of a centre…provides for a social structure, and a structure of meaning that is delimited or marked out by boundaries" (Jenks 2003, 15) that allows for the reconstitution of thresholds and transitive spaces. Life at the gym is juxtaposed against the work disciplines of a modern capitalist system with its "affective walls." I postulate that a lifestyle that entails physical exertions, perspiration, blood, and pain is an embodied kind of liminality which is absent in the monotony of a capitalist, knowledge-based economy in which most participants submerge their lives. Csordas (1994a, b, 269) defines embodiment as "a methodological standpoint in which bodily experience is understood to be the existential ground of culture and self, and therefore a valuable starting point for their analysis." In differentiating between the phenomenological and semiotic body, Csordas argues social actors experience embodiment through movements. The embodied experience is constantly subjected to re/interpretation by both the practitioner and audience. In this book, I focus on how the constant repetition of somatic movements creates the embodied experiences in the men. When asked about his motivations behind leaving his country for an extended period of 2 years to train in Muay Thai, Henry, 25, a Swedish professional fighter, comments:

> I needed a change in my life. I was bored. I worked as a security guard 3 years and before that I was in the army. I was bored... And I always loved to try [being a professional fighter] so I figured why not try do it professionally.

For some men, immersing themselves in the gym does not help to resolve personal existential crisis like the one vocalised by Henry. For these men, the gym constitutes a break from work, a liminoid experience. Turner (1982) offers the term liminoid to describe experiences that have some of the characteristics of liminality but are playful and optional events. The men's narratives often bifurcate between the liminal and the liminoid, blurring the boundaries between the two.

The existential quality of this communitas for the men lies in not only their temporal stay at the gym but also the constant grinding down of physical bodies as men engage in training and sparring matches. This somatic culture, constructed in opposition to a capitalist, productive lifestyle, exists at the margins and interstices of structure. Resonating with leisure studies, martial arts can be constructed as being ideologically opposite from work in a capitalist society that furbishes its workers with monetary remunerations (Dunning and Rojek 1992; Elias and Dunning 1986; Ladd and Mathison 1999; Parker 1983; Rojek 2000; Turner 1982). This articulation of work and leisure existing dichotomously has its origins in the advent of the Industrial Revolution (Clarke and Critcher 1985; Thompson 1966). There is thus a need to examine the ramifications these historical, social, and structural changes have on individuals. In *The Civilizing Process: The History of Manners*, Elias (1978) explores how civilisation results in human behaviour being transformed in a particular manner. Elias's historical analysis of etiquette books and textual accounts highlights how between the Middle Ages and the eighteenth century, there were radical transformations in what was previous seen as socially acceptable forms of human interactions in myriad areas such as table manners, the use of cutlery, natural functions, blowing one's nose, spitting, bedroom behaviour, changing attitudes towards male and female relations, and aggression. Elias views such shifts in the everyday life as indicative of profound transformations in basic human relationships in which the boundaries of aversion and embarrassment were raised and heightened, and there exists an "invisible wall of affects which seems now to rise between one human body and another, repelling and separating" (2000, 60). This "affective wall" affecting the mental and social structures of individuals within society impacts spatial relations between one's body vis-à-vis other foreign bodies. This shift was facilitated by what Elias terms as "'instrument[s] of civilisation', a symbol of the transformation at work in man: an 'emotional wall' is beginning to arise between man and his own body" (Fontaine 1978, 247). Elias (2000, 60) cites the fork as an instrument that radically impacts the way individuals consume their food, and transforms existing "forms of relationship and conduct." Prior to using the fork, it was customary in the Middle Ages for food to be shared, individuals to take "meat with their fingers from the same dish, wine from the same goblet, soup from the same pot or the same plate." However, in today's milieu, because of this "invisible wall of affects" (2000, 60), individuals demonstrate aversion and embarrassment at the thought of contact with the hands and mouths of others.

Elias attributes this "invisible wall of affects" to social causes that originated in the aristocratic life at court where there existed a "strict hierarchical subordination and [people were] ruled by the need to please those who could dispense favour and honour" (Seigel 1979, 124) that became pervasive throughout society. This transforms what was previously perceived to be a psychological compulsion into a social one. As a result, individuals come to be increasingly regulated by societal norms and structures. This compulsion to be civilised in one's performative actions is imposed internally rather than externally, resulting in gradual changes in the individual's subconscious. In short, integral to the civilising process is the manufacturing of distance between bodies that is coupled with the multiplication of prohibitions and restrictions (Elias 1978). Of the latter, Elias (2000, 375) writes:

> Through the interdependence of larger groups of people and the exclusion of physical violence from them, a social apparatus is established in which the constraints between people are lastingly transformed into self-constraints. These self-constraints, a function of the perpetual hindsight and foresight instilled in the individual from childhood in accordance with integration in extensive chains of action, have partly the form of conscious self-control and partly that of automatic habit.

Of particular relevance to the genre of martial arts is how the civilising process entails the pacification of society at both the physical level and the psychological level of affect (Elias 1978). The "affective wall" has a crucial role in the diminishing of violence in everyday interactions over the last 500 years as individuals exert a greater degree of self-control at the subconscious level over their actions. Civilisation is an ongoing process in which restrictions are placed upon the individual conduct with the purpose of attenuating excesses in violence, inequality, disorder, pleasure, and anarchy. *The Civilizing Process* thus posits a means by which observable, historical changes in the everyday life and mentalities can be linked to more macrostructural changes in society (Aya 1978). The move towards a refinement of social behaviour is thus the outcome of various processes such as increasing differentiation of labour and social stratification. As webs of interdependence between individuals get more elaborated and complex and the state's apparatus is able to systematically regulate acts of violence, "violent or crude forms of social behaviour gradually gave way to more controlled, 'civilised' conduct. This in turn entails a type of personality that is characterised by greater individuation, more empathy, stronger internalised controls and a better overall capacity for self-regulation, for mastery of emotion and deferment of immediate gratification" (Mouzelis 1995, 71).

Elias's concept of sportisation and mimetic events is also of relevance to this thesis that deals with the motivations for participation in this gym culture. For Elias (1971, 92), the term sportisation refers to the process that started in the eighteenth century, whereby organisations begin to define the "rules of sport-like recreations more precisely, strictly and explicitly, orientated around an ethos of 'fair play' and eliminating, reducing and/ or more strictly controlling opportunities for violent physical contact." In addition, to regulate the sporting arena, new organisational structures and bureaucratic positions such as referees were established (Van Bottenburg and Heilbron 2006). As such, Elias (1986, 151) views sportisation to mirror the "character of a civilizing spurt comparable in its overall direction to the 'courtisation' of warriors where the tightening rules of etiquette played a significant part" given that sportisation necessarily requires the strict cultivation of self-regulation and discipline amongst its participants. However, if sportisation results in the total absence of violence, there will likely be little allure for individuals to either take part in or observe such sporting events. Furthermore, contemporary empirical evidence suggests that the process can also operate in reverse. As Elias (1978, 186) argues, "The civilizing process does not follow a straight line" and there exist numerous intersecting movements, shifts, and spurts in myriad directions. One notable example would be MMA, an esoteric and eclectic mix of unarmed combat styles that had its genesis on 12 November 1993 (Van Bottenburg and Heilbron 2006; Downey 2007). In stark contrast to Elias's conjuncture that there will be a figurational shift towards sportisation, MMA, often touted as a no-holds-barred fight, has attracted much political backlash over its perceived excessive violence and barbarity (Van Bottenburg and Heilbron 2006). One way to account for these disparities is to view these events as being regulated, akin to "mimetic events" that occur in a "social enclave where excitement can be enjoyed without its socially and personally dangerous implications" (Elias and Dunning 1986, 90). These mimetic events fulfil an important function of generating tension, the demand of which can be said to be proportional to the extent of monotony in one's everyday life. Therefore, mimetic events are required to generate "the rise of an enjoyable tension-excitement, as the heart-piece of leisure enjoyment" (Elias and Dunning 1986, 88). Dunning (1999) later elaborates how sports are particularly suited for this "quest for excitement" (Elias and Dunning 1986, 3) because sports are associated with two other components, motility and sociability. Motility refers to the pleasures derived from submerging oneself in activities to escape from work disciplines, while sociability refers to the satisfaction derived from social interactions. In both cases, the emphasis in upon how sports provide an environment that is constructed in opposition to the modern, rationalised work environment. Yet the irony of the situation is that these men, in their quest to be free from rationalised work discipline, are immersing their bodies into the rigid discipline of the gym, abstaining from particular activities and foods. Shilling (2005, 117) remarks on how because sport can be both a "differentiated field that both rationalises and provides escape" for people and "an escape into rationalised life," some individuals experience "genuine tension and even irreconcilable conflict between the rationalised and transcendent possibilities of sport." Sport encapsulates this fundamental tension between human impulses towards play and work, at times blurring the boundaries as to what constitutes play or work.

Within the confines of the gym, the "affective wall" between individuals that is generated by societal norms and regulations is broken down during training. Individuals learn to put aside inhibitions and actively transgress this "affective wall" and trespass into the personal spaces and bodies of their opponents as the participants inscribe onto their opponents' bodies the force of their punches and kicks. Paul's comment of how he initially thought Muay Thai "was kind of violent [but] it does not feel violent anymore," is reflective of how the men have to be socialised to set aside the "civilising process" in their quest to be fighters. Given that existing societal norms regulate the use of violence against others, sparring can be seen as a liminal activity. This is especially the case for Norwegians like Michael and Sigurd, 27, a car mechanic, since knockout sports are banned in Norway. Michael comments on how he has to go to Sweden or places where "the politicians are [not] pussies" if he wishes to participate in competitions. For these Norwegians, sparring is liminal not only because it goes against the civilising process but also because it is illegal. It was only recently, in December 2014, that the Norwegian parliament overturned the "Knockout Law." This law criminalises any sports that involve the use of knockouts to either score points or win (McGrady 2014). Being a participant in this somatic culture requires one to normalise these acts of violence as well as relearning how to utilise the senses to engage another human being in a fight. Kelvin normalises the undercurrent of potential violence lurking in Muay Thai as being similar to other aspects of everyday life.

L.L   Have you been only doing Muay Thai or…
Kelvin   No. Been doing things like grappling, Jiu-jitsu, boxing, Muay Thai… kind of like everything
L.L   Everything? So what attracted you to doing all these?
Kelvin   I think it is kind of like testing yourself? There are a lot of team sports where you can rely on other people. But for these sports it is just one on one. When you test yourself. Makes you tougher… It is all about competing! Being competitive! So that was what attracted me to these sports.

Another strategy used by the men is to downplay the violence rampant in a match and allude to how it is an intellectual exercise. Ivar, for example, uses the metaphor of three-dimensional chess to describe sparring matches and comments that the appeal of fighting is that "everything you can do, someone can do it as well." Likewise, when I asked Jack what goes through his mind when he is in the ring and whether he thinks of punching his opponent, Jack, who was quick to rebut me, says:

No, of course not. It's the tactical stuff in MMA. Nothing emotional. You play the intellectual game man! You go in with a game plan based on your strength and your opponents' weaknesses.

At another level, the men are quick to dispel any suggestions that they are on a quest for authenticity. When I broached the notion that they had come here for the authentic experience, Wan was quick to dismiss this. He says:

> You think I would want to stay in a Muay Thai gym run by Thais? Sure it is authentic. The trainers are all Thai. They do not speak English. The living conditions are shit. You sleep on the floor with the other Thai orphans, treated like shit…. Fuck man here at least the boss is a foreigner. He makes sure that your needs are taken care of, makes sure that the Thais work for their money.

Rather than framing their sojourn in Thailand as being a quest for the authentic, the men view it as a journey to learn Muay Thai, a martial art which they appreciate for its efficiency and combat effectiveness. For example, Karl rationalises his decision to go to Thailand because this is where one gets the best training. He explains that the teachers here have been "fighting since they were in their diapers" and that Muay Thai as taught in other countries does not focus on elbows and knees. Karl's motivations for coming to Thailand echo the sentiments of most of the men. This focus on instrumental rationality is in keeping with the way in which the men draw upon various scientific discourses to regulate their bodies and bodily regimes. Instrumental rationality refers to actions that are the result of an actor's conscious and deliberate assessment of relative benefits and costs vis-à-vis other possible alternatives (d'Avray 2010; Ritzer 2006; Weber 1978). These martial arts aficionados justify their passion for Muay Thai by drawing upon a vocabulary demarcated by rationality, describing Muay Thai as being a practical form of self-defence and asserting that "it works." These perspectives regarding the practicality and efficiency of Muay Thai are further reinforced from their own experiences as well as those gleaned from the media. Insofar as these narratives point to a desire to learn a combat-effective martial art while ignoring its ritual traditions, learning the authentic Muay Thai is not a foremost priority. One of the few exceptions to this is Jack, who chooses to define himself as an untypical American, as the vignette below highlights:

L.L   So why Muay Thai then? Have you learnt other martial arts before this?

Jack   Yeah! I started BJJ [Brazilian Jiu-Jitsu] when I was about fourteen. In America, Jiu-jitsu has become very popular as everyone wants to do it. So it has lost much of its cultural meaning. But Muay Thai, it still has much deep deep cultural meaning. You know it is still the traditions that they did 100 years ago is still being practised today you know. People still do the Wai Khru, pay respects, you sip water from the other coach...

L.L   So in America Muay Thai is not popular?

Jack   Respect is not popular in American martial arts. It is all about showing how tough you are and I am the best, you know. And here there is a lot more respect for the art and for the...

L.L   Yeah and the Wai and...Cause I notice that amongst all the guys, except maybe you, me and Deep are more respectful to the Ajarns [teachers] as well?

Jack   Yeah, yeah. Exactly!

In addition, remarks about how relatively inexpensive the costs of accommodation and training are in Thailand are prevalent. While these remarks can be perceived as yet another example of calculative rationality, they are also indicative of how Muay Thai has been deeply embedded within global cultural flows (Appadurai 1996, 33) that provide some of the impetus behind foreigners coming to Thailand to train Muay Thai. In *Warrior Dreams: The Martial Arts and the American Imagination*, Donohue (1994a, b) offers some insight into the ramifications these transnational flows have for martial arts and how this consumption is linked to the "essentially emotional and aesthetic pull" (2002, 66) of martial arts in general. My participants, with their emphasis on calculability and efficiency, differ from Donohue's respondents in that martial arts, for them, are not imbibed as part of popular culture or surreal fantasy. These comments also illuminate a darker aspect of globalisation, of how nation states are intertwined within a world system that segregates nation states into core, semi-periphery, and peripheral countries. The latter are often manipulated and at times exploited by the former for their resources (Wallerstein 1990, 1998, 2004). These men are able to indulge in what some would consider a middle-class lifestyle, not fretting about being away from home over an extended period of time, precisely because of the existing constellations of power which structure world systems. For the majority of the men, the cost of training and accommodation in Thailand is relatively inexpensive. The men's relatively higher class statuses back home allow them to engage in martial disciplines overseas and perceive such activities as departing from their societal norms. Muay Thai, a discipline integral to Thai culture, is perceived to be liminal for these men not only because it is foreign but also because fighting is not part and parcel of the lifestyle that the men partake of back home.

These structural changes that posit a radical break from the mundaneness of everyday life bring about a liminal state. This quest for liminality may answer the question of why in a milieu where there is little need for martial arts as a form of self-defence, martial arts remains popular. People are willing to pay money to subject their bodies to pain and injury, while simultaneously attempting to master techniques that can inflict pain and injury on others. While structural in nature, liminality is simultaneously experienced by the individual through rituals and symbols that create cognitive dissonances (Turner 2008). Turner is credited as one of the pioneers who directed scholarly attention towards issues of embodiment (Howson and Inglis 2001). My research shows how liminality is an inherently embodied experience. Donohue (2002, 73) characterises martial arts as an autotelic activity (an activity that individuals engage in because they find the activity rewarding in itself) that engages practitioners on myriad levels such that different individuals with varying skills and competency can still benefit from it. Csikszentmihalyi (1990) argues that this sort of activity produces a state which he refers to as "flow." "Flow" is the pleasure derived from the sense of being immersed in the activity. Individuals are constantly subjected to increasingly challenging tasks that demand a complete absorption at both the physical and intellectual levels as they immerse themselves in a particular activity. Caught up in the flow, intense concentration on the activity at hand means individuals do not have the leisure to either ponder or worry about problems or irrelevant issues as "self-consciousness disappears" and spatial and temporal distortions occur (1990, 71). Csikszentmihalyi asserts that individuals in the flow are said to be in a transcendent state, restricted neither by self-awareness/reflexivity nor by normative constraints. In attempting to tease out the nuances of flow, Csikszentmihalyi argues that certain activities are conducive to flow and the achievement of optimal experience is easier due to the way in which these activities are framed:

> They have rules that require the learning of skills, they set up goals, they provide feedback, they make control possible. They facilitate concentration and involvement by making the activity as distinct as possible from the so-

called "paramount reality" of everyday existence... for the duration of the event, players and spectators cease to act in terms of common sense, and concentrate instead on the peculiar reality of the game. Such flow activities have as their primary function the provision of enjoyable experiences. Play, art, pageantry, ritual, and sports are some examples. Because of the way they are constructed, they help participants and spectators achieve an ordered state of mind that is highly enjoyable (1990, 72).

Parallels can be drawn to sports and martial arts, which can be said to be a flow activity par excellence (cf. Blake 1996; Higdon 1992; Saville 2008; Sheehan 1992; Thrift 2005). Regardless of the different reasons why individuals take up martial arts and the way in which their individual subjectivities construct martial arts, I argue that through the act of breaking down the "affective wall" between individuals, as well as by immersing the self in a new activity/culture, martial arts can create a liminal space, that provides "a sense of discovery, a creative feeling of transporting the person into a new reality...push[ing] the person to higher levels of performance, and lead[ing] to previously undreamed-of-states of consciousness. In short, it transform[s] the self by making it more complex. In this growth of the self lies the key to flow activities" (Csikszentmihalyi 1990, 74). The men refer to this mental state as "being in the zone." This terminology is also commonly employed by the American cage-fighters in Holthuysen's (2011) study. For some men "being in the zone" is a fundamental pillar in their game plan. Michael and Karl were discussing about Karl's fighting style in his amateur boxing matches, and Karl mentioned that unlike some guys who got all hyped up and do crazy shit, he just becomes quiet and rather focused:

Michael	In the zone?
Karl	I guess so. I don't talk that much nor think about my fight. I don't like to worry too much. Some guys get really uptight and they worry a lot. I also don't like to get too tense either. I just like to be calm, relax, and don't think of things to make sure I have a stable mental state. I don't have a lot of other things in my mind cause if you got other things in your mind, you will mess up the fight.
Michael	You are scary man! You go all quiet and then you fuck your opponents up right? [laughs] When I am training I am also like in the zone! Totally focused!

Csikszentmihalyi locates this flow as the synergistic outcome of the body engaging in harmonious or rhythmic movements such as those found in dance, athletics, sex, yoga, and martial arts and the resulting unity of mind and body as the intentionality of the mind is translated into embodied actions in the world (1990, 95). Loh (2010) also cautions against privileging either the body or the mind to the exclusion of the other but highlights the need to transcend this constructed dualism. Based on the above vignettes, the feeling of flow then appears to be central to understanding some of the motivations behind practitioners' continued involvement in martial arts (Donohue 1994a, b; Holthuysen 2011; Satterlund 2006). More importantly, it points to the need to move away from purely discursive discussions of martial arts and theorise about issues of embodiment and the senses.

Here, I have shown how the gym exists as a liminal space that stands apart from the everyday life of the participants due to its isolated location as well as to the social norms and regulations that promote an almost exclusively masculine ethos. I argue that this liminality is best comprehended through the transformative processes to which the men subject their bodies and their sensory experiences. I offer the concept of embodied liminality, which emphasises how the structural disjunctures from everyday create a state of liminality that is best comprehended through the body and the senses. Issues of embodiment thus lie at the crux of my analysis. In Chap. 4, I shall endeavour to illustrate how being a good fighter necessitates more than being able to adapt to this culture that privileges masculinity and bodily capital but also entails reconfiguration of one's senses and a relearning of techniques of the body.

References

Appadurai, A. (1996). *Modernity at large: Cultural dimensions of globalisation.* Minneapolis: University of Minnesota Press.

Aya, R. (1978). Norbert Elias and "The civilizing process". *Theory and Society, 5*(2), 219–228.

Bierly, M. M. (1985). Prejudice toward contemporary outgroups as a generalized attitude. *Journal of Applied Social Psychology, 15*(1), 189–99.

Bishop, R., & Robinson, L. S. (1999). Genealogies of exotic desire: The Thai night market in the western imagination. In P. A. Jackson & N. M. Cook (Eds.), *Genders, and sexualities in modern Thailand.* Thailand: Silkworm Books.

Blake, A. (1996). *The body language: The meaning of modern sport.* London: Lawrence and Wishart.

Bourdieu, P. (1977). *Outline of a theory of practice* (R. Nice, Trans.). Cambridge: Cambridge University Press.

Bourdieu, P. (1984). *Distinction: A social critique of the judgement of taste* (R. Nice, Trans.). London: Routledge and Kegan Paul.

Bourdieu, P. (1990a). *The logic of practice.* Stanford, CA: Stanford University Press.

Bourdieu, P. (1990b). *In other words: Essays towards a reflexive sociology* (M. Adamson, Trans.). Stanford, CA: Stanford University Press.

Bourdieu, P. (1998). *Practical reason.* Cambridge: Polity Press.

Britton, D. M. (1990). Homophobia and homosociality: An analysis of boundary maintenance. *The Sociology Quarterly, 31*(3), 423–439.

Brown, J., & Graham, D. (2008). Body satisfaction in gym-active males: An exploration of sexuality, gender and narcissism. *Sex Roles, 59*(1–2), 94–106.

Bruch, H. (1997). Body image and self-awareness. In C. Counihan & P. Van Esterik (Eds.), *Food and culture: A reader.* London: Routledge.

Burstyn, V. (1999). *The rites of men: Manhood, politics, and the culture of sports.* Toronto, Canada: University of Toronto Press.

Butler, J. (1990). *Gender troubles. Feminism and the subversion of identity.* New York: Routledge.

Celsi, R. L., Rose, L. R., & Leigh, T. W. (1993). An exploration of high-risk leisure consumption through skydiving. *Journal of Consumer Research, 20*(1), 1–23.

Clarke, J., & Critcher, C. (1985). *The devil makes work: Leisure in capitalist Britain.* London: MacMillan.

Coakley, J. (2001). *Sport in society: Issues and controversies* (7th ed.). Boston, MA: McGraw Hill.

Connell, R. W. (1995). *Masculinities.* Berkeley: University of California Press.

Cook, N. M., & Jackson, P. A. (1999). Introduction/desiring constructs: Transforming sex/gender orders in twentieth-century Thailand. In P. A. Jackson & N. M. Cook (Eds.), *Genders, and sexualities in modern Thailand.* Thailand: Silkworm Books.

Craib, I. (1998). *Experiencing identity.* London: Sage Publications.

Crosset, T. (1999). 'Male athletes violence against women: A critical assessment of the athletic affiliation, violence against women debate. *Quest, 51*(1), 244–57.

Crossley, N. (2006). In the gym motives, meanings and moral careers. *Body and Society, 12*(3), 25–50.

Csikszentmihalyi, M. (1990). *Flow. The psychology of optimal experience.* New York: Harper and Row.

d'Avray, D. L. (2010). *Rationalities in history. A Weberian essay in comparison.* Cambridge: Cambridge University Press.

Davies, C. (1982). Sexual taboos and social boundaries. *American Journal of Sociology, 87*(5), 1032–1063.

Donohue, J. J. (1994a). *The martial arts and the American imagination.* West Port, CT: Bergin and Garvey.

Donohue, J. J. (1994b). *Warrior dreams: The martial arts and the American imagination.* West Port, CT: Bergin and Garvey.

Donohue, J. J. (2002). Wave people: The martial arts and the American imagination. Combat, ritual, and performance. In D. E. Jones (Ed.), *Anthropology of the martial arts.* London: Praeger.

Douglas, M. (1966). *Purity and danger.* London: Routledge.

Downey, G. (2007). Producing pain: Techniques and technologies in no-holds-barred fighting. *Social Studies of Science, 37*(2), 201–226.

Dunning, E. (1999). *Sport matters.* London: Routledge.

Dunning, E., & Rojek, C. (1992). Introduction: Sociological approaches to the study of sport and leisure. In E. Dunning & C. Rojek (Eds.), *Sports and leisure in the civilising process: Critique and counter-critique.* London: Macmillan.

Elias, N. (1971). The genesis of sport as a sociological problem. In E. Dunning (Ed.), *The sociology of sport: A selection of readings.* London: Frank Cass.

Elias, N. (1978). *The civilising process: The history of manners.* New York: Urizen Books.

Elias, N. (1986). An essay on sport and violence. In N. Elias & E. Dunning (Eds.), *Quest for excitement: Sport and leisure in the civilizing process.* Oxford: Basil Blackwell.

Elias, N. (2000). The civilising process. In: E. Dunning, J. Goudsblom, & S. Mennell (Eds.), *Sociogenetic and psychogentic investigations* (E. Jephcott, Trans.). Cornwall: Blackwell.

Elias, N., & Dunning, E. (1986). *The quest for excitement in leisure: Sport and leisure in the civilizing process.* Oxford: Basil Blackwell.

Ewert, A. W. (1994). Playing the edge: Motivation and risk taking in a high altitude wilderness like environment. *Environment and Behaviour, 26*(1), 3–24.

Fontaine, S. (1978). The civilising process revisited: Interview with Norbert Elias. *Theory and Society, 5*(2), 243–253.

Foster, G. M. (1986). South sea cruise: A case study of a short-lived society. *Annals of Tourism Research, 13*(1), 215–238.

Giddens, A. (1991). *Modernity and self-identity: Self and society in the late modern age.* Palo Alto, CA: Stanford University Press.

Gilman, S. (2002). Black bodies, white bodies: Toward an iconography of female sexuality in the late nineteenth century. In S. Jackson & S. Scott (Eds.), *Gender: A sociological reader.* London: Routledge.

Goffman, E. (1971). *The presentation of self in everyday life.* Harmondsworth: Penguin.

Green, K. (2011). It hurts so it is real: Sensing the seduction of mixed martial arts. *Social and Cultural Geography, 12*(4), 377–396.

Greenberg, D. F., & Bystyrn, M. H. (1982). Christian intolerance of homosexuality. *American Journal of Sociology, 88*(3), 515–548.

Hall, S. (1996). Ethnicity: Identity and difference. In G. Eley & R. G. Suny (Eds.), *Becoming national: A reader.* New York: Oxford University Press.

Heaven, P. C. L., & Oxman, L. N. (1999). Human values, conservatism and stereo- types of homosexuals. *Personality and Individual Differences, 27*(1), 109–18.

Herek, G. M. (2000). Sexual prejudice and gender: Do heterosexuals' attitudes toward Lesbians and Gay Men differ?". *Journal of Social Issues, 56*(1), 251–66.

Higdon, H. (1992). Is running a religious experience? In S. J. Hoffman (Ed.), *Sport and religion.* Champaign, Il: Human Kinetics.

Holthuysen, J. (2011). *Embattled identities: Constructions of contemporary American masculinity amongst mixed martial arts cagefighters.* Unpublished doctoral thesis, Arizona State University, United States of America.

Howson, A., & Inglis, D. (2001). The body in sociology: Tensions inside and outside sociological thought. *Sociological Review, 49*(3), 297–317.

Jackson, P. A. (1999). Tolerant but unaccepting: The Myth of Thai "Gay Paradise". In P. A. Jackson & N. M. Cook (Eds.), *Genders, and sexualities in modern Thailand.* Thailand: Silkworm Books.

Jackson, P. A., & Sullivan, G. (1999). A Panoply of roles: Sexual and gender diversity in contemporary Thailand. In P. A. Jackson & G. Sullivan (Eds.), *Lady Boys, Tom Boys, Rent Boys: Male and female homosexualities in contemporary Thailand.* New York: The Haworth Press, Inc.

Jenks, C. (2003). *Trangression.* New York: Routledge.

Johansson, T. (1996). Gendered spaces: The gym culture and the social construction of gender. *Young, 4*(3), 32–47.

Kay, J., & Laberge, S. (2002a). The 'New' corporate habitus in adventure racing. *International Review for the Sociology of Sport, 37*(1), 17–36.

Kay, J., & Laberge, S. (2002b). Mapping the field of 'AR: Adventure racing and Bourdieu's concept of field. *Sociology of Sport Journal, 19*(1), 25–46.

Kite, M. E. (1984). Sex differences in attitudes toward homosexuals: A meta-analytic review. *Journal of Homosexuality, 10*(1), 69–81.

Kreager, D. A. (2007). Unnecessary roughness? School sports, peer networks, and male adolescent violence. *American Sociological Review, 72*(5), 705–724.

Ladd, T., & Mathison, J. (1999). Muscular Christianity: Evangelical protestants and the development of American sport. *Grand Rapids: Michigan: Baker Books..*

Leach, E. (1967). *Rethinking anthropology.* London: Althone Press.

Loh, H.L.L. (2010). *Transcending dichotomies: Embodied intersections of self, structure and agency amongst Singaporean Chinese males.* Academic Exercise-Department of Sociology, Faculty of Arts and Social Sciences, Singapore: National University of Singapore.

Mauss, M. (2006)[1935]. Techniques of the body. In: N. Schlanger (Ed., Introduced) *Techniques, technology and civilisation*. New York: Durkheim Press.

McGrady, J. (2014, December 17). Norway legalises boxing after three-decade Ban. *The Boxing Tribute*.

Messner, M. A. (1990). Boyhood, organized sports, and the construction of masculinities. *Journal of Contemporary Ethnography, 18*(1), 416–44.

Messner, M. (1992). *Power at play: Sports and the problem of masculinity*. Boston, MA: Beacon Press.

Mills, W. (1940). Situated actions and vocabularies of motive. *American Sociological Review, 5*(6), 904–913.

Morin, S. F., & Garfinkle, E. M. (1978). Male homophobia. *Journal of Social Issues, 34*(1), 29–47.

Morrison, T. G., Parriag, A. V., & Morrison, M. A. (1999). The psychometric properties of the homonegativity scale. *Journal of Homosexuality, 37*, 111–26.

Mouzelis, N. (1995). *Sociological theory: What went wrong? Diagnosis and remedies*. London: Routledge.

Muir, K. B., & Seitz, T. (2004). Machismo, misogyny, and homophobia in a male athletic subculture: A participant-observation study of deviant rituals in collegiate rugby. *Deviant Behavior, 25*(1), 303–27.

Parasecoli, F. (2005). Feeding hard bodies: Food and masculinities in men's fitness magazines. *Food and Foodways, 13*(1), 17–35.

Parker, S. (1983). *Leisure and work*. London: George Allen and Unwin.

Rantala, K., & Lehtonen, T.-K. (2001). Dancing on the tightrope: Everyday aesthetics in the practices of shopping, gym exercise and art making. *European Journal of Cultural Studies, 4*(1), 63–83.

Reid, G. (1994). That's why I go to the gym: Sexual identity and the body of the male performer. *Theatre Journal, 46*, 477–88.

Ritzer, G. (2006). *McDonaldisation the reader* (2nd ed.). Thousand Oaks, CA: Pine Forge Press.

Robinson, K. (1996). Of mail-order brides and "Boys' Own" tales: Representations of Asian-Australian marriages. *Feminist Review, The World Upside Down: Feminisms in the Antipodes, 52*(1), 53–68.

Rojek, C. (2000). *Leisure and culture*. Britain: Macmillan Press.

Sabo, D. (1994). Pigskin, patriarchy and pain. In M. Messner & D. Sabo (Eds.), *Sex, violence, and power in sports: Rethinking masculinity*. Freedom, CA: Crossing Press.

Sakalli, N. (2002). The relationship between sexism and attitudes toward homosexuality in a sample of Turkish College Students. *Journal of Homosexuality, 42*(1), 53–64.

Sanday, P. R. (1990). *Fraternity gang rape. Sex, brotherhood, and privilege on campus*. New York, NY: New York University Press.

Satterlund, T. D. (2006). *Fighting for an authentic self: An ethnographic study of recreational boxers*. Unpublished doctoral thesis, University of North Carolina, North Carolina.

Saville, S. J. (2008). Playing with fear: Parkour and the mobility of emotion. *Social and Cultural Geography, 9*(1), 891–914.

Seigel, J. (1979). Review: The civilizing process: The history of manners by Norbert Elias. *The Journal of Modern History, 51*(1), 123–126.

Sheehan, G. (1992). Playing. In S. J. Hoffman (Ed.), *Sport and religion*. Champaign, IL: Human Kinetics.

Shilling, C. (1993). *The body and social theory*. London, Newbury Park: Sage.

Shilling, C. (2005). *The body in culture, technology and society*. London: Sage.

Spencer, D. C. (2009). Habit(us), body techniques and body callusing: An ethnography of mixed martial arts. *Body and Society, 15*(4), 119–143.

Stebbins, R. A. (1999). Serious leisure. In E. L. Jackson & T. L. Burton (Eds.), *Leisure studies: Prospects for the twenty-first century*. United States of America College, PA: State Venture Publishing Inc.

Storer, G. (1999). Rehearsing gender and sexuality in modern Thailand: Masculinity and male-male sex behaviours. In P. A. Jackson & G. Sullivan (Eds.), *Lady Boys, Tom Boys, Rent Boys: Male and female homosexualities in contemporary Thailand*. New York: The Haworth Press.

Thompson, E. P. (1966). *The making of the English working class*. New York: Vintage Press.

Thompson, E. H., Grisanti, C., & Pleck, J. H. (1985). Attitudes towards the male role and their correlates. *Sex Roles, 13*(7/8), 413–427.

Thrift, N. (2005). *Non-representational theory: Space, politics and affect*. London: Routledge.

Turner, V. (1974). *Dreams, fields and metaphors*. New York: Cornell University Press.

Turner, V. (1982). *From ritual to theatre: The human seriousness of play*. New York: Paj.

Turner, V. (2008). Liminality and communitas. In M. Lambek (Ed.), *A reader in the anthropology of religion* (2nd ed.). United Kingdom: Blackwell.

Van Bottenburg, M., & Heilbron, J. (2006). De-sportization of fighting contests: The origins and dynamics of no holds barred events and the theory of sportization. *International Review for the Sociology of Sports, 41*(3), 259–282.

Van Gennep, A. (1960). *The rites of passage*. London: Routledge and Kegan Paul.

Wacquant, L. (2004). *Body and soul, notebooks of an apprentice boxer*. Oxford: Oxford University Press.

Wallerstein, I. (1990). World-systems analysis: The second phase. *Review (Fernand Braudel Centrer), 13*(2), 287–293.

Wallerstein, I. (1998). The rise and future demise of world-systems analysis. *Review (Fernand Braudel Centrer), 21*(1), 103–112.

Wallerstein, I. (2004). *World-systems analysis: An introduction.* Durham: Duke University Press.

Weber, M. (1978). In G. Roth & C. Wittich (Eds.), *Economy and society.* Berkeley: University of California Press.

Wheaton, B. (2000). Just do it: Consumption, commitment, and identity in the windsurfing subculture. *Sociology of Sport Journal, 17*(1), 254–274.

Young, K., White, P., & McTeer, W. (1994). Body talk: Male athletes reflect on sport, injury, and pain. *Sociology of Sport Journal, 11*(1), 175–94.

CHAPTER 4

Knowing Your Body

Abstract Furthering the leitmotif of the centrality of the body in influencing the somatic, masculine ethos of the gym, I argue that being a successful fighter entails not only sensitised awareness and knowledge of one's body that is gleaned through careful observation and subjecting one's body to particular figurations of physical regimes, but also a reconfiguration of the senses. However, the body of a fighter comes at the cost of the excessive stress of these bodily regimes and age will definitely take a toll on these fighters.

Previously, I described the ethnographic reality of the gym, detailing the centrality of the body in influencing the somatic, masculine ethos of the gym. I highlight how liminality is an embodied experience by detailing the various aspects that give rise to a liminal experience. While the ability to perform the identity of a masculine fighter allows one to adapt to life at the gym, one must also be able to demonstrate one's credentials as a fighter within the confines of the boxing ring. Furthering this thread of embodied experiences, I argue that being a successful fighter entails not only sensitised awareness and knowledge of one's body, which is gleaned through careful observation and subjecting one's body to particular figurations of physical regimes, but also a reconfiguration of the senses. I analyse these bodily frames of behaviour vis-à-vis the sensory performance required of a fighter and the physical limitations of the body. The accumulation of bodily knowledge in relation to the life course of a fighter is the organis-

© The Editor(s) (if applicable) and The Author(s) 2016
Loh H.L.L, *The Body and Senses in Martial Culture*,
DOI 10.1057/978-1-137-55742-1_4

ing structure of this chapter, linking the journey of an aspiring fighter with that of a fighter past his prime.

The impetus behind this analysis is due to the phenomenon of how Muay Thai fighters often hold their bodies in particular poses when being photographed. These postures not only exist as signifiers of martial arts but also require the individual to possess a cultivated awareness of his body, and the sensory feedback, gleaned through immersing oneself in this somatic culture, that imperceptibly adjusts the way in which he stands. The fact that these poses remain surprisingly consistent amongst fighters of different nationalities is of sociological significance. The favourite pose is the typical Muay Thai stance, with feet shoulder width apart, to ensure stability when kicking or getting kicked, and arms raised to the face with fists clenched, ready to throw a punch or guard against attacks. This bodily posture that challenges the surroundings, ready to actively throw a punch or a kick, stands in stark contrast to Young's (1980) analysis of the feminine body as being socialised to be withdrawn from the social and physical environment. Insofar as these bodily dispositions (Bourdieu 1977) of Muay Thai actively challenge and dominate spaces, forcing the perception of self/thought away from the body, the projection of one's senses towards the world (see Merleau-Ponty 2002) as somatic dispositions are constitutive of masculinity. The gym functions as a social institution that shapes a particular habitus amongst the fighters. Within the habitus, the individual acquires particular practices relating to thought, action, and perception. These cognitive and embodied dispositions are the result of individuals reacting with larger social structures and Bourdieu (1977) theorises them to be self-perpetuating and sustaining. At the gym, bodily dispositions are sustained, reinforced, and perpetuated via the bodily techniques of martial arts, which in turn, necessitates a particular body schema.

In addition to the bodily dispositions that reflect the *techniques du corps* of Muay Thai, individuals often adorn their bodies with expressive equipment (Goffman 1971) that are signifiers for doing Muay Thai when they pose for photographs. These include hand wraps and boxing gloves, but the most important signifier that differentiates the men from mere boxers is the Muay Thai shorts. The men often train topless, taking the opportunity to show off their lean and muscular physique at the gym, and pose bare-chested in photographs. Muscularity is often a signifier for masculinity (Amico 2001). An analysis of casual shots taken by the men highlights how they continuously adopt these poses to emphasise their identity as masculine Muay Thai fighters. Furthermore, it can be argued that photographs, which capture selective slices of social reality, are to a certain extent staged and do not reflect an objective but a subjective reality. This subjective reality, hinting at the subjectivities and positionalities of Muay Thai practitioners, is reflected through the bodies of individuals, which is the focus of this chapter. Positionalities refer to how the men situate themselves vis-à-vis other fighters and the manner in which their bodies have already been socialised by their native cultures. I argue that Muay Thai, as a traditionally masculine martial art, is a medium by which individuals enact the presentation of their selves in the everyday.

Techniques of the body, thus, do not simply refer to the internalising of particular martial arts techniques but also point to a reconfiguration of the senses. This reconfiguration is not only due to the requirements of particular martial arts but is also indicative of a need to break away from the civilising processes (Elias 1978) that have led to increasing suppression of violent impulses and have disciplined the body and the senses in the direction of greater self-control. In *Techniques of the Body*, Mauss (2006 [1935], 83) constantly reiterates the role of culture in constructing the body as a technical object, and perpetuating particular techniques of the body. Culture is heavily embroiled in the way one uses the body. By analysing bodily frames of reference, I further build on the notion of embodied liminality by showing how individuals are socialised to use their bodies in this case study of martial arts culture. However, subjecting their bodies to such relentless physical discipline comes at a price as their bodies inevitably start to break down. Next, I will describe some of the strategies employed by the men in dealing with issues of injuries as well as the onset of old age. These strategies need to be contextualised in relation to the masculine ethos of the gym and the intimate, somatic knowledge of their bodies possessed by the men.

Reconfiguring the Senses, Transforming the Body

In *The Production of Space*, Lefebvre (2002, 133) was concerned with "logico-epistemological space, the space of social practice, the space occupied by sensory phenomena, including products of imagination such as projects, projections, symbols and utopias" and how the production of space is the result of particular socio-historical relations. Extending my previous argument of how embodied liminality arises from the men learning to put aside the inhibitions of the civilising process, the gym itself is a liminal space because its activities do not contribute to the economic sphere of production; furthermore, being situated within transnational flows, it is a "local space" with "global attractions" (see Chap. 5). The latter refers to individuals frequenting Thailand because it is constructed as the site of effective and "authentic" Muay Thai. In his *Critique of Everyday Life*, Lefebvre's (1991) radical questioning of the everyday in modernity arises from the way in which historical developments, and political processes, such as capitalism and the rise of bureaucracy, have impacted societies.

In this chapter, I analyse the social space of the gym, paying heed to the way in which spaces are used at the gym, the spatial practices this space constitutes and expresses, and the men's lived experiences. Martial arts training, involving specific embodied practices, can theoretically be conceived as creating or producing a particular social space. At the gym, spatial practices involve the men subjecting their bodies to physical regimes, learning the techniques of the body, and reconfiguring their senses to be a successful fighter. I argue that the success of a fighter is partially due to his ability to imaginatively perceive the spaces around him as he spars. This imagining is constructed via one's ideas, thoughts, memories, existing discourses on martial arts (see Donohue 1994a, b; Chap. 5), and the somatic, masculine gym culture. In this section, I will focus on the phenomenological aspect of the gym and how the success of a fighter requires a reconfiguration of the way we use our senses and a transformation of the body's corporeal schema. Corporeal schema refers to embodied knowledge which the individual acts upon by utilising his body and senses in a particular manner to view the world (Crossley 2001, 123). This perspectival grasp of viewing the world via the body is developed through the repetition of cultural practices such as the gym's regimes, which I will elaborate upon.

SENSORY DISCUSSION

Non-verbal social interactions permeate the highly sensorial lived spaces of the gym. This extract from my field notes highlights the gym's sensorial nature:

> Prior to the start of every training session, individuals will often go for a short run or jog around the lake. By the time I reach the gym after my run,

I am already breathing heavily and my body is drenched with sweat. In the background, the stereo blasts loud Thai music or English pop music. Some guys are already on the mats, doing their warm-ups by skipping for about 20 minutes. The sound of the skipping ropes slicing through the air at high speeds, the 'thud' sound as the ropes hit the ground, and feet landing, at times silently, on the mats have a particular rhythm that is a countermelody to the music from the stereos.

As the training progresses, beads of perspiration mark out the perimeter of the boxer's movements and shortly after, the red mats of the gym are drenched with sweat and the smell of sweat starts to envelop the gym. As punches and kicks are thrown around, beads of perspiration trail down the men's bodies, their breathing get louder and more ragged and waves of heat start to emit off their bodies.

From the foam rubbery feel of the mats where one skips and shadow boxes, I then enter the Muay Thai ring. Subjected to the constant rigours of training, the canvas floor of the ring and the other protective equipment are worn out, the faint odour of perspiration all that remains. The sound of gloved fists lashing out at the boxing mitts has now replaced the sound of the skipping ropes. As the Ajarns shout out the commands, each fighter pounds the mitts in accordance with their own speed and force, producing a cacophony of sounds. Ajarn Noy put on his pads and asked me to punch, kick, knee, block and elbow him. Whenever he feels and experiences a particularly good execution of technique, he will shout loudly with phrases such as, "Yes sir", "Yes! Yes!", "Good! Again! Harder!" His shouting certainly contributes to the somatic atmosphere of the gym!

In what follows, I will briefly sketch out these sensorial dimensions and how they help to construct the lived spaces of the gym. These sensorial data illustrate how spatial practices and representations of space come together to create the gym as a specific lived space.

Whether one spars with another participant or is under the direct tutelage of an Ajarn, considerable interactional work maintains the social order. Aural work is crucial for participants to assess each other's proficiency through their exhalations and utterances (cf. Hockey 2006). Aural work also occurs when individuals await instruction from their trainers, and as the above extract demonstrates, the instructor's shouts help to motivate the learner. These "soundscapes" provide crucial information about how one should train, and react (see Rodaway 1994). In the above vignette, constant reference was also made to the olfactory dimension, about the perspiration and odour that engulf the gym. This fetid odour that is emitted by bodies in training is part of the gym's "smellscapes"

(Classen et al. 1994, 97). As physical sensations, these odours assault the senses, and contest normative assumptions of the body's integrity as being discrete and impermeable. The men often joked about being "under siege" from pungent smells and expressed revulsion when their own bodies are marked by the fetid odour of others. Smells, embedded with a culture's particular social order, are imbued with meanings. Synnott (1993, 190) argues how odour is a signifier for one's physical presence and is a "symbol of the self." Likewise, pungent smells that are the result of their training are evidential of the men's identity as fighters. It is only in the context of the gym that the smells of stale sweat, dirt, and grime are seen as something self-affirming, given how these smells reaffirm and substantiate the salience of the men's identity as boxers. Smells, inundated with social meanings (see Hockey 2006; Hockey and Allen-Collinson 2009; Loh 2010; Low 2009), help to sustain the social order of a particular lived space because of their communicative function within conceived spaces. Smells, as a form of tacit knowledge (Polanyi 1983), can invoke embodied memories, and vice versa because neurologically, information from the olfactory system is transmitted to both the cortex and the limbic system. The latter, as a primitive part of the brain, allows for the unconscious evocation of memory, emotions, and behaviours (Hubbard and Ramachandran 2003; Malaspina et al. 2002). In his ethnographic work of MMA fighters, Spencer (2012, 48) details his informants associating the stale smell of sweat and astringent odour of muscle liniment with training and the gym. One of his respondents actually commented on how "there is a smell that you get wrestling and training, and that smell gets [me] in the fight mode" (2012, 49).

At the level of spatial practices, ocularcentric work occurs via what Sudnow (1972) terms "the glance." Individuals scrutinise their opponents' bodily postures, and facial expressions, such as grimaces, to ascertain the effectiveness of their blows. A good fighter should ideally possess "expressive control" over his external "signalling" (Goffman 1971, 59-60) so that his opponents will not have visual cues to the effectiveness of their punches. In the conversation below, Aaron was commenting how Jack's facial features are a dead give-away:

Aaron   When you smile I know I got you man! You are starting to hurt
        from my punches!
Jack   Really?
Aaron   Yes, I can tell. In San Francisco, there is this thing they call the
        wooden man. No expressions when fighting at all man! Totally

> different from how you spar! Every time I hit you good? Bam! I
> know I have you when you smile! [laughs]

The ability to predict one's opponent's attacks is facilitated not only by
these visual cues but also by the way in which a fighter positions or orien-
tates his hands, shoulders, elbows, and feet. Sensory feedback allows the
fighter to develop the "feel" of his opponents, and sparring is a mechanism by which this skill is honed. The men often talked about how they
would like to constantly spar with different coaches since each instructor has a different style, and "feel." Individuals will also have to learn to
compensate for differences in height and weight. Ajarn Noy's body is able
to communicate to the men his bodily capital not simply through sight
but through sparring sessions. The men often talked about "sparring with
Noy... [as being on a] totally different level and dimension!" As a novice,
I learnt how to ignore the bruises that were beginning to form on my
body, the sweat pouring down into my eyes, and concentrate solely on my
opponent (see Wacquant 2007). Individuals learn to visualise their knees
and elbows as extensions of their selves. Muay Thai, often affectionately
known as the art of eight limbs, calls upon neophytes to reconceptualise
the way they view their own bodies. As fighters utilise particular Muay
Thai techniques, re-enacting and performing specific postures and gestures (Feher 1987, 159), they are immersing themselves in the conceived
spaces of what Muay Thai is to them. Simultaneously, the men's initial
normative ideas of what Muay Thai entails are also being challenged as
their bodies are being socialised into performing particular bodily techniques of Muay Thai taught and practised at the gym. During training,
individuals are also socialised to utilise visualisation techniques. When one
is raining blows on a punching bag, one learns to view the inanimate bag
as a living thing, and that the blows are hitting vital areas of the body
such as the liver, kidneys, ribs, and jaw. Ironically, while these visualisation
techniques attempt to embody the inanimate, individuals may deliberately disembody and dehumanise their opponents within the boxing ring.
Similar to the way in which scientific discourses dismember the patient's
body (Young 1997), rendering it vulnerable, and malleable to scientific
discourses (Foucault 1990) which circumvent the individual's agency,
this disembodying of their opponent's bodies into discrete components
projects a map of targets to punch. I suggest this visualisation technique
allows individuals to throw off the inhibitions of the civilising process.
Individuals thus learn to simultaneously oscillate between embodying and
disembodying other individuals, as well as objects, in the gym.

While the body as a visual map of targets can be discursively constructed, Leder (1990, 23) reminds us that "the body is always a field
of immediately lived sensation...its presence is fleshed out by a ceaseless
stream of kinesthesias, cutaneous and visceral sensations." The haptic is
the "combination of tactile and locomotive properties... [which] provides
information about the character of objects, surfaces and whole environ-
ments as well as our own bodies" (Rodaway 1994, 48). It unifies the
senses as bodies circulate within these spaces. Acknowledging that cultural
paradigms and existential knowledge impact one's bodily movements,
Merleau-Ponty (1962) argues that "reversibility" is important to understanding the bidirectional, embodied relationship the body has with the
world. Reversibility refers to the act of fighters' actively touching other
bodies and objects, which in turn entails their also being touched by these
objects. For example, in punching the boxing mitts, somatic information
is transmitted between the fighter and the trainer. This sensorial feedback
results in the issuing of new commands and the modification of the pace
and intensity of the interaction. I have illustrated how each of the various
senses has a role to play in this somatic culture, but the reality is that all
the senses come into play simultaneously. Although cultures often construct a hierarchy of the senses (Howes 2004a, b), within the boxing ring,
this differentiation of the senses disappears. The vignette below highlights
how lived spaces, which entail intimate involvement of the senses, throw
into question the feasibility of viewing each form of sensory feedback as a
discrete category, and the process of "reversibility":

> There will be attempts to maintain constant eye contact, watching Ajarn
> Lai's movements as he calls out for me to execute different punches or kicks.
> The quality of the punches I throw is not only measured by our eyes but the
> impact of the punches on the pads. This impact, experienced between the
> fighter and trainer, forges a temporary relationship between the two. After
> some time, Ajarn grabs hold of my leg and twists it in a particular position so
> that I will be forced to use my hips. Ajarn does this to me a couple of times,
> holding my body and forcing it into the correct position, forcing me to use
> the hip, and hand movement to accelerate the power of my kicks.

Within the sensoryscape of the gym, there is a synergistic effect as
the senses inform haptic movements. Muay Thai is a dynamic process
of embodiment because of the centrality of movements in triggering
"sensory activity that the consciousness in turn experiences as feelings"

(Tangen 2004, 21). Men who are forced to take a short hiatus from training due to their injuries often remarked how they needed time to get back into the "zone," into the "groove." James talks about how he needed time to "get back into it [Muay Thai], to feel that burning sensation in the shoulders, and that satisfying feeling as your punch whacks your opponent hard!" However, embodying these techniques is only one component of the habitus of a Muay Thai fighter. Rhythm and timing are also essential to the art. Goodridge (1999, 43) defines corporeal rhythm in human physical performance as a "patterned energy-flow of action, marked in the body by varied stress and directional change; also marked by changes in the level of intensity, speed and function." My auto-ethnographic narration as a beginner attempting to learn something as basic as punching a boxing bag exemplifies how this rhythm requires intense, corporeal socialisation.

> When I am asked to do padwork, what would appear to be one of the easiest tasks always eludes me. The ajarn will first push the bag, making it swing in a pendulum-like motion and once the bag comes within range, fire off a salvo of attacks. I often miss, pause or just stop the bag's oscillation only to restart its motion again later. I have difficulty gauging the appropriate distance, the timing needed to initiate my attack, and how much I should step forward so that my punch coincides with the bag's approach. Rather than a loud "bam", which resonates in the gym whenever the ajarn's punches hit the target, mine is a soft "thud". It is only after three weeks of training that my ability to sense the 'correct' distance improves.

Rhythms permeate these lived spaces of Muay Thai and are evident when one participates in a boxing match. Lefebvre's *Rhythmanalysis* (2004) elucidates how by taking into account the body's natural rhythms social space has its own rhythm. Rhythms exist in the lived realities, consisting of "movements and differences within repetition" (2004, 90), and individuals are often not conscious of how they are embedded in "this unity of diverse relations whose aspects are subordinated to action towards the external world, orientated towards the outside, towards the Other and to the world, to such a degree that they escape us" (2004, 77). My ethnographic research seeks to unveil these existing rhythms prevalent at the gym. Despite appearing to be spontaneous, Lefebvre argues that this repetition involves a measure, which is to say, a "law, calculated and expected obligation, a project" (2004, 8) that imprints its rhythm onto a particular space. Prior to the commencement of the match, the fighter performs the Wai Khru Ram Muay, a ritualistic dance that honours one's trainers and gym. The fighters often perform this dance according to their own rhythms and paces, appearing calm and serene. Observations at two local Muay Thai matches sensitise me to this rhythm. A match, which consist of five rounds, follows a patterned rhythm: a slow start, as fighters circle their opponents, sizing up their opponents' measure by throwing punches before increasing in pace and intensity as the rounds progress. This rhythm is experienced by the audience as towards the later rounds, thunderous cries and shouts rock the stadium each time a blow is scored. The audience's response, as a verbal manifestation of the rhythms of a Muay Thai match, resonates with the rhythms of the fighter as they strive for supremacy. Henry's personal experiences in the ring also correspond with my observations. He comments:

> For example in a fight, first two rounds pretty easy going you know? You feel out your opponent and then 3rd and 4th rounds you really get on it, try to kill each other and then the 5th round starts to slow down.

This rhythm is embodied because it is at the most primordial level that it is first experienced through the visceral body. Teasing out the nuances of this tempo, Wacquant (2007, 148), in like manner, elucidates how "the level of violence fluctuates in cycles according to a dialectic of challenge and response" and is indexed against the fighter's emotional and mental states.

Participants who are professional fighters often talk about how their bodies know that they have an upcoming fight.

Paul   Do you know how many people, they work 9 to 5 job for 30 years, they eat breakfast every day same time, they go work exact same time, and they pick up their kid exact same time? Life is just a routine for them. For me, every 3 months [prior to a match], I get to go find something out of myself. That's intense man! Really is intense! And you know you try, you try to deal with this in ways. When I was in Singapore [competing], you try to tell yourself, "I been doing this well". This is okay, just any other day, just any other week but on the week of the fight you body just knows. Human beings fight for a million of years, now is for prize money but it always been fighting, surviving right. Your body just knows, you know, tells you something is gonna happen this week. As it gets closer and closer to the event, you hate that feeling? But you love it you know at this moment! What's gonna happen, your future is undecided. Maybe God knows what's gonna happen, maybe a higher being knows what's gonna happen but I don't know what is gonna happen.

L.L   You said that you body just know? Means what, your body tends to...?

Paul   Yeah you just wake up... your body will tell you on Monday that the fight is on Saturday. On Monday, you body is like hey man, you wake up, you are a little bit more keen, a little more aware of things going on around you and your body just changes man ... That's kind of like excitement! Like I said, you don't know that... the future for this particular moment in your life, no one know what is gonna happen. I love that feeling.

The above extract is significant because it succinctly reiterates the pertinent points of this chapter. I have argued that embodied liminality arises as a consequence of the civilising process. This civilising process impacts societal relations, and the way in which individuals come to perceive the relationship they have with their bodies and those of others. The construction of the gym as a liminal space is also influenced by larger sociohistorical changes such as the institutionalisation of sports. The gym, as a lived space, is thus dependent on the discursive and embodied construction of martial arts, and particular bodily techniques. Permeating these spaces is a rhythm around which bodies and social interactions revolve. Paul's narrative of how his body "knows" when a match is coming can be seen as a conflux of the above factors, and is also indicative of the arduous training that embodiment entails. Rhythms also structure the gym's regimes. Towards the end of the week, as bodies tire and succumb to the rigorous training schedule of training twice a day, individuals may not turn up for training and even those who do may not be as energetic and enthusiastic. Conversely, after Sunday, the designated rest day, individuals start off the week with renewed vigour with the sounds of shouting, the gloves hitting the pads resonating loudly during training.

To summarise, I demonstrated how the body's rhythms, body callusing, and sparring are crucial in constructing the defining characteristics of the gym as a lived space. Insofar as the somatic and masculine gym culture helps to situate these lived spaces, I argue that issues of embodiment and liminality must be analysed vis-à-vis the civilising process. By analysing the relationship between bodies and particular cultural practices via phenomenology, I elucidate the processes of embodiment, and the ramifications that gym culture has. However, the assumption that bodies are always sturdy enough to withstand the rigours of training needs to be problematised. This embodied liminality is a transitory phrase due to the aging body and the accumulation of injuries sustained by the fighters over time. Individuals are forced out of this liminal state and reaggregated back to society partially because of their mortal bodies. In the next section, I shift my analytical focus towards bodies that have been constructed as disabled, and the strategies employed by the men to deal with their bodies when they obstinately refuse to submit to and comply with the regimes at the gym.

THE AGING BODY AND PAIN

The daily physical regimes to which the men subject their bodies as they strive to master new techniques of the body and be transformed into better fighters come at a price. The men often talk about using scientific developments to improve their bodies. Scientific discourses, which the men internalise, are premised upon the principle of productivity and efficiency. The allure behind the use of scientific discourses is that it promises "limitless performance" (Hoberman 1992, 25) by "subordinating the body completely to the will of the rational mind" (Cashmore 1998, 84). Yet such training, which forces the body to operate at its limits to "elicit positive adaptational responses" (Shilling 2005, 110), marks the flesh. The body constantly treads a fine line between optimal performance and physical breakdown. There is a contradiction between discourses that inscribe ideals of wholeness, the body's integrity, and the lived realties in which injuries contest these discursive constructions by rendering the body vulnerable and susceptible. In addition to injuries that may severely curtail the lifespan of a fighter, training regimes and strict schedules may force fighters to forgo activities such as birthday celebrations, weddings, and other celebrations. These sacrifices may negatively affect their physical and psychological well-being (Evans et al. 2003; Flynn 1998; Hargreaves 1994; Sparkles 1999; Toole 1998). Paul's reflexive comments illustrate this:

L.L   What are some of the opportunity costs that you made over your years as a professional fighter who travels constantly?

Paul   The cost to your family life, your personal life is tremendous. I miss lots of moments. You know my only brother? He has a daughter and when she was born I was getting ready for a fight... I wasn't there when she was born... Moments like that. Well looking back now, would it been a big difference to have missed two days of practice to go see her? 'Cause she might be the only child in the family...She is now a wife, having kids... things like that. Where am I now? Where are all we at? Thailand. Away from my family, away from my friends but I believe somewhere someplace down the line, this will be the reason why I win. If you don't do that, won't do it, then you are not gonna make it unless you are born with superhuman skills...

The demands that the men subject their bodies to unveil the contradiction inherent within the discourse of the modern sporting body. Despite the belief that modernity has "colonised nature" (Giddens 1991) through the use of scientific advances such as performance-enhancing drugs and supplements, the body "remains a mortal, limited phenomenon" (Shilling 2005, 111). The training regime at Kwaan-saa-maat Gym has taken its toll on the men, with many suffering from various joint injuries, and sprains. In addition, most of the men, who come from temperate climates, were not acclimatised to the humid, tropical monsoon season, and started falling sick.

> Vernon talked about how it was raining the last few days and he didn't really train yesterday as well. He said, "Guys are like falling sick... it keeps raining man... me, James and Henry are all on antibiotics." Karl also commented that it is something that has been going around the gym, everyone is coming down with a throat infection.

The spread of this particular illness was exacerbated by the nature of martial arts training, which generally involves a lot of body contact, and the use of communal sporting equipment.

Even before their arrival at Kwaan-saa-maat Gym, the bodies of the men have already been marked by their involvement in martial arts. Oates's (1987, 25) observation of how "boxing is more about getting hit than it is about hitting" underscores the importance of scrutinising the physical aspects of fighting. The muscular physique of the men, the broken bones, sprains, and bruises experienced by their bodies are not only reflective of the rigorous training to which they have subjected their bodies but also narrate their trials and tribulations as fighters, a non-verbal testimony to the professional fights in which they have participated. The interview below highlights how the men's personal stories as fighters are imprinted on their bodies:

Stefan   When are you going to fight again?
David   I don't know man... my knee and this shit [points to his shoulders]
Stefan   How much time before you will recover from that knee?
David   Honestly? I don't know man...I had so many broken bones from all my fights... my knees, ribs, hand, collarbone were all broken in my previous fights... I think I am having so many problems, like my current broken knee, because of cutting weight to meet the weight categories... cutting weight [is] really fucking me over...

Mauss (2006) notes that culture plays a role in mediating the way one uses one's body, detailing how growing up is an embodied process of socialisation. Brooks (1989, 1) originally used the term *storied bodies* to discursively examine the role that bodies play in literature, and how bodies are pieces of "work in progress... [The concept of storied bodies] concerns the relation of the body to narrative: how bodies come to be inscribed in narratives and narratives inscribed on the body." The concept, storied bodies, discursively examines the interlinkages between bodies and narratives. In this book, I alter this concept and utilise storied bodies not in the discursive sense but to detail the centrality of embodiment within this somatic culture. Storied bodies become a lens for comprehending how encapsulated within the men's bodies are narratives of somatic experiences. Not only do the men learn how to embody martial disciplines by reconfiguring their senses and bodily movements, but also the injuries sustained in the course of their training continue to remind them of their past experiences, and their mortality. Yet, pain inscribed onto the body can be positive and reaffirming. Pain, as a biological response to external stimulus, forces the individual to respond or prevents further injury or suffering (Melzack 2001; Schiefenhövel 1995). Sensory feedback modifies adaptive responses in reaction to the changing environment. Within these lived spaces, the men deliberately attempt to increase their pain thresholds, and normalise the pain experienced. One mechanism by which they normalise the pain is to perceive pain as temporary, telling themselves that the pain that they would have experienced if they had not been training hard would be multiplied. For example, when I asked David for advice on how to avoid flinching when a punch is thrown at my face, he says:

> You realise that a punch is less dangerous to you when you see it coming, versus closing your eyes pretending it is not coming. That could hurt you so much more. You have to see it. When I see the punch coming right at my face, I can put my chin down and absorb it with my body [raise his fists to his cheeks and tilt his neck downwards] If you keep your chin down, then the body absorbs the shock. I can eat good shocks to my face and still not be taken.

Pain, arising from the utilisation of particular muscles not often used in the everyday, is also an important avenue by which individuals come to embody martial arts. This type of pain, as a form of body callusing (Spencer 2009), is embraced by fighters because it is a reminder of their progress, their journey into martial arts, and that they are becoming better by using the "proper" muscles (cf. Spencer 2012). Jack nonchalantly commented on how when he was doing kickboxing in Sweden, he would get the guys to punch him in the forehead as a form of training. In an activity where injuries are the norm, what is of greater sociological interest is how the men deal with their injuries and manage their relationship with their injured, aging bodies.

My ethnographic data helps to further elucidate the culturally specific and subjective experience of pain in the sporting realm (see Allen-Collinson 2005; Hockey and Allen-Collinson 2007; Howes 2004a, b; Loland et al. 2006; Sparkes and Smith 2003). Merleau-Ponty (1962) argues that individuals project their consciousness into the world around them. In contrast, pain is the catalyst that results in individuals focusing exclusively on the materiality and fragility of their bodies. Scarry (1985, 32–35) argues that in moments of intense pain:

> as the body breaks down, it becomes increasingly the object of attention, usurping the place of all other objects...destroy[ing] a person's self and world, a destruction experienced spatially as either the contraction of the universe down to the immediate vicinity of the body or as the body swelling to fill the entire universe. Intense pain is also language-destroying: as the content of one's world disintegrates, so the content of one's language disintegrates; as the self disintegrates, so that which would express and project the self is robbed of its source and its subject.

The men are constantly reminded of the injuries sustained during training as pain restricts and limits their range of movements.

L.L	So how did you injure yourself in the first place?
Alvin, 22, Danish	Actually I injured myself while I was practising MMA back home in Denmark. So actually I have been injured for like 5 weeks now? More actually...
L.L	And yet you are still able to train?
Alvin	Yeah. I can still do some techniques... I can't do push-ups but I can do the jabbing, punching and everything? So it depends on what move I have to make for my shoulder...As long as the pain doesn't flare up, I guess I should be fine? Maybe after my fight back home, I will take a break for a month or something if I can. [Laughs] I like to train so it is hard not to train even if you are injured.
L.L	So you know the injury is there but you have to adapt after the pain?
Alvin	Yeah but sometimes I still have to know when to say stop because while I can take some [pain], I still got a limit for how much [pain] I can take. But shoulder injuries are fucked up man... I mean if you break an arm it heals but dislocate a shoulder it will always be a problem. Always going to be... this shoulder [pain] is always going to be with me.

Despite attempts to regulate, rationalise, and discipline the body, the body is able to defy such rational body projects through pain. Pain is a stark reprimand and reminder that our identities are constituted and restricted by the potentialities of the physical body. Bodily techniques are not only embodied but pain, which has the ability to return to haunt the self many years later, will always be a visceral testimony to the carnal costs of training. The men often attempt to normalise the pain experienced by weaving it into an ongoing narrative about their identities as masculine, stoic fighters. Most of the men were adamant about continuing their training despite the injuries sustained and developed strategies, such as varying their exercise regimes, to work around the limitations of their bodies. This is exemplified by how Jack constantly reiterates the need to continue training even when one is injured:

L.L   How do you feel when you can't train because of your injury?

Jack   I believe you can always train something. Maybe not if you are really sick. If you are injured you can always do some kind of training! You should always do some kind of training. I don't really believe you can't do any unless you are paralysed or something.

L.L   I think it depends on the kind of injury? When I sprained my lower back, I really cannot walk! I have difficulty walking down the stairs and everything.

Jack   But you can do those rubber band exercises. There is always some kind of exercise you can do. Unless it is that extreme then of course you should not train. But if it is an arm or leg you could do something.

These vocabularies of motives (Mills 1940) employed by the men, to justify why they persist in their training despite their injuries, unite them under the gym's ethos of stoic masculinity. When I continued to train despite suffering from a sprained ankle, the men were more amiable and forthcoming towards me. My performance of machismo and masochism was positively received by the men precisely because it is in accordance with the gym's somatic and masculine culture. My experiences show that to be a man at the gym is to learn to wear the injuries as a silent badge of pride. The men, in their portrayal of stoic masculinity, often use the phrase "suck it up and endure bro! You will get stronger!" as a means to motivate each other to not only become better fighters but also to present a stoic front despite the rigours of training. Corresponding to the study of professional footballers conducted by Roderick et al. (2000), my findings indicate how the status of injured fighters, and the connotations associated with injury and pain, can be comprehended only by locating these shared meanings within the specific configurations of social interaction found in different sports. Pain, in directing one's consciousness back into the body, also illuminates how bodily techniques require an ongoing process of socialisation. Pain, as a form of sensory feedback, forces the individual to possess heightened somatic awareness and knowledge. Injured individuals need to work through their injuries by reconfiguring their bodies into new bodily techniques. Due to a previous fight in which he "grounded and pounded" his opponent, and knocked him out despite his hand being broken in two different places, Wan commented that his hand is "not normal anymore." Since that incident, Wan uses hand wraps and wrist guards to protect his hand. He also laments how he has to either learn to punch in a way that does not aggravate his injury or focus on using his other limbs as part of his "game plan."

However, underneath this veneer of performing their identity as masculine fighters lurks a suppressed narrative that is often silenced. In reshaping their physique, the men's bodies embody not only pain but also the loneliness that arises from their aging or injured bodies. The body breaking down from the rigours and strains of training focuses one to orientate one's consciousness towards the body, stressing the individual's inability to continue to be involved in the ongoing social interactions at the gym. Henry, who was feeling depressed over his inability to train due to an injury sustained from competing at a local Muay Thai match, commented how the gym is "like a prison when you cannot train. No money to drive out and having to eat only meals at the gym is depressing, man. Sometimes you want to just give up... nothing to do when you don't train." Henry later elaborates:

Henry   It is a little bit depressing right now because I am injured. I cannot even lift weights because my hand is fucked. Now, I am just trying to maintain my weight. I lost 2–3 kg the last month and that is pretty depressing.

L.L   Why is it depressing?

Henry   Because I want to stay in heavyweight division.

L.L   Are there times when you feel down because you can't train?

Henry   Yeah it is very depressing. You feel like crying almost every day because you can't train. It is tough, to see everyone else training and you are sitting there doing nothing.

Karl, who was down with flu the last couple of days, also echoed these sentiments:

L.L   How do you feel when you are unable to train?

Karl   Like shit. It sucks! I stay in my room watching everyone else train, you know? It does get to you but you just got to endure. I am only 22 years old. It does piss me off but I got a long time to learn. I always want to improve but your body has its limits.

In Honkasalo's (1998, 36) study of the embodied experience of chronic pain, her informants describe their "chronic pain experience through a peculiar spatiality." Individuals with chronic pain often encounter estrangement as pain restricts their mobility, creating new boundaries and restrictions. This liminal space created by pain parallels the narratives of the men's storied bodies.

These feelings of depression that arose from a body restricted by pain are further exacerbated by the liminality of the gym. Previously, I argued that the liminal experience at the gym is constructed through its isolated location, social mores, and norms. These factors reinforce the liminal experience because individuals who fail to conform are not only marginalised but left with few other avenues of social interaction in this "short-lived society" (Foster 1986). These narratives of angst and despair highlight one of the unintended consequences of this embodied liminality. Fighters whose bodies have reached their physiological limits due to the demands of competitions and training possess bodily capital that is highly sought after at the gym. Injured bodies are testimonies to the sacrifice, blood, and toil inherent in martial arts. Green's (2011, 378) ethnographic study of an MMA community demonstrates the role of pain in providing a common ground, a "shared intimacy" between the men, allowing a community to form. Yet my participants, in embodying the masculine ethos of a fighter, also express ambivalence towards their ailing bodies. Injured bodies require rest, and precious training time is forsaken. Injuries may also be the result of competing against a more experienced fighter, and one's insufficient training. In this situation, the men feel even more compelled to train harder, but their injured bodies deny them this opportunity. For some men, they may experience despair and helplessness (cf. Spencer 2012). The paradox encapsulated within this discourse is further intensified because constant training is deemed crucial to being a successful fighter. Paul's comment on how "If you try to get to the top, you better be in the gym hustling. You want to stay in the game, you better be in the gym hustling" exemplifies this discourse.

Despite the constant exhortations to push their bodies to the limits, and drawing upon scientific discourses, regimes, and innovations to improve and prolong their lifespan as fighters, these men are also painfully aware of their bodies' mortality. The cultivated awareness of how their bodies function allows the men to be highly sensitised to the curtailing of their bodily motions due to the onset of injuries and age. Venkat views this process as his body slowly "accumulating all the injuries in [his] ankle, shin guards, and shoulder blades," necessitating longer recovery times as the frequency of his body breaking down increases. Kelvin, who was also a personal trainer in the past, illustrates the point of how although the men subscribe to scientific discourses, they too are aware of the limitations of science in thwarting the mortality of the body:

L.L   You previously mentioned how your body breaks down. Would
         that be one of the factors that result in you not practising Muay
         Thai in the future?
Kelvin   Yeah. If you do martial arts or things that are hard on your body,
         you have to eat right, sleep enough. You have to look after your
         body, making sure that it is well rested. Otherwise you would
         have to give up [training in martial arts] because your body
         wouldn't be able to do it anymore. People get old, get injured...
L.L   So when will you know when your body cannot be pushed
         anymore?
Kelvin   Maybe when you start to feel sore all over your body or an injury
         that doesn't heal? Then you know it is time to rest... maybe time
         to stop?
L.L   So it is very important to know your body?
Kelvin   Yeah, you have to listen to your body. You don't always train
         through pain. You have to listen to your body and if your body
         is feeling sore you have to rest. There is a limit to how far eat-
         ing healthy and using supplements can help you when you are
         injured or getting old.

While all the men expressed their wish to continue doing Muay Thai even till they are old, they recognise the physical exertions and opportunity costs of practising martial arts. Professional fighters like David, Henry, Paul, and Venkat realise that with each passing year, their "expiry date" as fighters draws near. Their deteriorating bodies, occasionally stricken with pain, constantly remind them of previous battles, and increasingly become less physiologically responsive to the demands the men place on them.

L.L   Do you see a time where you foresee you stop fighting
         professionally?
David   Sure. Everyone has to face that path.
L.L   Due to age? Or injuries?
David   It's a mix of both I mean I am not getting any younger and with
         old age comes slowing down. I may be smarter than some of
         these guys but I know well that conditioning and passion makes

up for that. My passion may also be burning out. You are going up against someone living his dream, he's young, fast. He may not be as gifted but he is giving 300% and in terms of conditioning, he may even have an upper hand. At one point I was a young guy, trying to take out guys like me now, guys that has been in the game for long. Now I learnt as much as I can, train as much as I can, to prevent that 19-year-old guy from taking me out. It is not cool to be old but I am hardworking and I love the game!

L.L How about physical injuries?

David I have broken bones in my ribs, jaw, ankle, toes, and thumbs. I broke my nose three times, had a knee operation, and neck surgery. Injuries definitely play a factor [in not competing professionally]. I guess each injury has a story to tell and it either keeps me going or it slows me down.

Other participants also acknowledge that because of the demands that martial arts place on one's physical body, their current devotion to martial arts is heavily dependent upon their leisure time, and the particular stage of their life course which they are at. Ray, who is going to law school soon, even comments how being a Muay Thai fighter, with a battered body, is certainly not going to be conducive to his future identity as a working professional.

Ray What might I achieve from this [Muay Thai]? Is this going to be something I am going to use? At the end of the day, I see myself being a professional, a lawyer. And honestly I don't reckon I have the time... Maybe I would be able to do a bit of the bags at the gym or do an occasional session but I wouldn't be able to be... I wouldn't want to be worrying how am I going to get to Muay Thai every day when I got, you know, a demanding high pressure job... At the moment I am young and I got a lot of free time is a good thing to do.

L.L Okay. Because Muay Thai is quite high impact, the thought of having injuries can also be a deterrent right? I can't see myself practising or doing Muay Thai when I am in my 40s or 50s.

Ray Exactly! I wouldn't want to go and do [Muay Thai] when I am 35, 40 and I am a senior professional and I got a responsible job.

> I wouldn't want to come into work the next day with a black eye because I have been doing Muay Thai. At the moment, I can get away with it because I am 19. A black eye from doing Muay Thai? Fair enough. A legitimate activity for someone my age, but I don't think I will be able to get away with it when I am older. Imagine you see a 40-year-old man in a nice suit, a good briefcase, with a black eye... It wouldn't do wonders for my image!

Previously, I drew upon Elias's (1978) work on the civilising process to substantiate my argument that in the context of modern societies, where restrictions and taboos are placed upon bodily contact with others, Muay Thai, which transgresses societal norms of personal space, can be seen as a liminal activity. To further expound upon this argument, these vignettes, showcasing an ethnographic slice of the men's social reality, highlight the body's failure to respond to repeated calls for exertion and strain, and reflect on how larger social norms influence the disciplining of the body. Ray's comment illustrates how when he is in his forties, at the peak of his career as a working professional, his body needs to be disciplined in a way that is to him antithetical to Muay Thai training.

To conclude, this chapter continues the leitmotif of somatic knowledge and culture, and elaborates on the men's lived experiences. I discuss bodily frames of behaviour that are socialised, displayed, and perpetuated through sensory performance and the limitations of the aging body. By situating the social construction of space within the larger socio-historical milieu, I demonstrated how fighting can be a liminal activity for the men and how through a reconfiguration of the senses, embodiment works from the inside out, as it were, rather than being imposed on the body. Reiterating the fact that the body inevitably eludes attempts to rationalise and quantify it, I point out that the assumption of bodies always being able and healthy is inherently problematic in a culture that subjects the body to such excessive stress. Yet, rather than unveil these contradictions about the body's abilities, the strategies employed by the men serve to mask and perpetuate the contradictions at the gym. Having dealt with the phenomenological production of the gym's spaces, in the next chapter I analyse the ways in which sensorial knowledge is impacted by transnational flows. I question how fighters learn to recalibrate their sensory know-how at the global level, and how this has ramifications on the constructions of the gym's lived spaces.

REFERENCES

Allen-Collinson, J. (2005). Emotions, interaction and the injured sporting body. *International Review for the Sociology of Sport, 40*(2), 221–240.

Amico, S. (2001). 'I Want Muscles': House music, homosexuality and masculine signification. *Popular Music, 20*(3), 359–378.

Bourdieu, P. (1977). *Outline of a theory of practice* (R. Nice, Trans.). Cambridge: Cambridge University Press.

Brooks, P. (1989). Storied bodies, or nana at last unveiled. *Critical Inquiry, 16*(1), 1–32.

Cashmore, E. (1998). Between mind and muscle (review article). *Body and Society, 4*(2), 83–90.

Classen, C., Howes, D., & Synott, A. (1994). *Aroma: The cultural history of smell.* London: Routledge.

Crossley, N. (2001). *The social body: Habit, identity and desire.* London: Sage.

Donohue, J. J. (1994a). *The martial arts and the American imagination.* West Port, CT: Bergin and Garvey.

Donohue, J. J. (1994b). *Warrior dreams: The martial arts and the American imagination.* West Port, CT: Bergin and Garvey.

Elias, N. (1978). *The civilising process: The history of manners.* New York: Urizen Books.

Evans, J., Davies, B., & Wright, J. (2003). *Bodies of knowledge.* London: Routledge.

Feher, M. (1987). Of bodies and technologies. In H. Foster (Ed.), *Discussions in contemporary culture no 1.* Seattle: Seattle Bay Press.

Flynn, M. (1998). Future research needs and directions. In R. Kreider, A. Fry, & M. L. O'Tooles (Eds.), *Overtraining in sport.* Champaign: Human Kinetics.

Foster, G. M. (1986). South sea cruise: A case study of a short-lived society. *Annals of Tourism Research, 13*(1), 215–238.

Foucault, M. (1990). *The history of sexuality* (Vol. II). New York: Vintage Books.

Giddens, A. (1991). *Modernity and self-identity: Self and society in the late modern age.* Palo Alto, CA: Stanford University Press.

Goffman, E. (1971). *The presentation of self in everyday life.* Harmondsworth: Penguin.

Goodridge, J. (1999). *Rhythm and timing of movement in performance.* London: Jessica Kingsley.

Green, K. (2011). It hurts so it is real: Sensing the seduction of mixed martial arts. *Social and Cultural Geography, 12*(4), 377–396.

Hargreaves, J. (1994). *Sporting females.* London: Routledge.

Hoberman, J. (1992). *Mortal engines.* New York: The Free Press.

Hockey, J. (2006). Sensing the run: The senses and distance running. *Senses and Society, 1*(2), 183–202.

Hockey, J., & Allen-Collinson, J. (2007). Grasping the phenomenology of sporting bodies. *International Review for the Sociology of Sport, 42*(2), 115–131.

Hockey, J., & Allen-Collinson, J. (2009). The sensorium at work: The sensory phenomenology of the working body. *The Sociological Review, 57*(2), 217–39.

Honkasalo, M.-L. (1998). Space and embodied experience: Rethinking the body in pain. *Body and Society, 4*(2), 35–57.

Howes, D. (2004a). *Sport, professionalism and pain*. London: Routledge.

Howes, D. (Ed.). (2004b). *Empire of the senses: The sensual culture reader*. Oxford and New York: Berg.

Hubbard, E., & Ramachandran, V. S. (2003). The phenomenology of synaesthesia. *Journal of Consciousness Studies, 10*(8), 49–57.

Leder, D. (1990). *The absent body*. Chicago: University of Chicago.

Lefebvre, H. (1991). *Critique of everyday life, translated by John Moore, with a preface by Michel Trebitsch*. London: Verso.

Lefebvre, H. (2002). The production of space. In J. D. Michael & F. Steven (Eds.), *The spaces of postmodernity. Readings in human geography*. Massachusetts, USA: Blackwell.

Lefebvre, H. (2004). *Rhythmanalysis. Space, time and everyday life* (S. Elden & G. Moore, Trans.). New York: Continuum.

Loland, S., Skirstad, B., & Waddington, I. (2006). *Pain and injury in sports: Social and ethical analysis*. London: Routledge.

Loh, H.L.L. (2010). *Transcending dichotomies: Embodied intersections of self, structure and agency amongst Singaporean Chinese males*. Academic Exercise-Department of Sociology, Faculty of Arts and Social Sciences, Singapore: National University of Singapore.

Low, K. E. Y. (2009). *Scents and scent-sibilities: Smell and everyday life experiences*. Cambridge Scholars Pub: Newcastle upon Tyne.

Malaspina, D., Coleman, E., Goetz, R. R., Harkavy-Friedman, J., Corcoran, C., Amador, X., et al. (2002). Odour identification, eye tracking and deficit syndrome schizophrenia. *Biological Psychiatry, 15*(10), 809–815.

Mauss, M. (2006)[1935]. Techniques of the body. In: N. Schlanger (Ed., Introduced) *Techniques, technology and civilisation*. New York: Durkheim Press.

Melzack, R. (2001). Pain and the neuromatrix in the brain. *Journal of Dental Education, 65*(12), 1378–1382.

Merleau-Ponty, M. (2000)[1962]. *Phenomenology of perception* (6th ed.) (C. Smith, Trans., with translation revisions supplied by Forrest Williams and David Guerriere). London: Routledge and Kegan Paul.

Merleau-Ponty, M. (2002). *Phenomenology of perception* (C. Smith, Trans.). London; New York: Routledge.

Mills, W. (1940). Situated actions and vocabularies of motive. *American Sociological Review, 5*(6), 904–913.

Oates, J. C. (1987). *On boxing*. Garden City, NY: Doubleday.

Polanyi, M. (1983). *The tacit dimension*. Garden City, New York: Doubleday and Company.

Rodaway, P. (1994). *Sensuous geographies: Body, sense and place*. London: Routledge.

Roderick, M., Waddington, I., and Parker, G. 2000. "Playing Hurt: Managing Injuries in English Professional Football." *International Review for the Sociology of Sport* 35(2): 165–180.

Scarry, E. (1985). *The body in pain: The making and unmaking of the world*. New York and Oxford: Oxford University Press.

Schiefenhövel, W. (1995). Perception, expression, and social function of pain: A human ethological view. *Science in Context, 8*(1), 31–46.

Shilling, C. (2005). *The body in culture, technology and society*. London: Sage.

Sparkes, A., & Smith, B. (2003). Men, sport, spinal cord injury and narrative time. *Qualitative Research, 3*(3), 295–320.

Sparkles, A. (1999). The fragile body-self. In A. Sparkes & M. Silvennoinen (Eds.), *Talking bodies: Men's narratives of the body and sport*. Jyvaskyla: SoPhi.

Spencer, D. C. (2009). Habit(us), body techniques and body callusing: An ethnography of mixed martial arts. *Body and Society, 15*(4), 119–143.

Spencer, D. C. (2012). *Ultimate fighting and embodiment. Violence, gender, and mixed martial arts*. New York: Routledge.

Sudnow, D. N. (1972). Temporal parameters of interpersonal observation. In D. Sudnow (Ed.), *Studies in social interaction*. New York: Free Press.

Synnott, A. (1993). *The body social: Symbolism, self and society*. London: Routledge.

Tangen, J. O. (2004). Embedded expectations, embodied knowledge and the movements that connect: A system theoretical attempt to explain the use and non-use of sport facilities. *International Review for the Sociology of Sport, 39*(1), 7–25.

Toole, M. (1998). Overreaching and overtraining in endurance athletes. In R. Kreider, A. Fry, & M. L. O'Tooles (Eds.), *Overtraining in sport*. Champaign: Human Kinetics.

Wacquant, L. (2007). The social logic of sparring: On the body as practical strategist. In J. Hargreaves & P. Vertinsky (Eds.), *Physical culture, power, and the body*. New York: Routledge.

Young, I. M. (1980). Throwing like a girl: A phenomenology of feminine body comportment motility and spatiality. *Human Studies, 3*(1), 137–156.

Young, K. (1997). *Presence in the flesh: The body in medicine*. Massachusetts: Harvard University Press.

CHAPTER 5

The Global Martial Circuit and Globalised Bodies

Abstract In this chapter, I elucidate, vis-à-vis the processes of globalisation, how martial arts are embedded within transnational flows and practices that simultaneously feed back into the embodied and discursive construction of martial arts. I appropriate Appadurai's concept of "-scapes" and offer the term "martialscape" to describe the dynamic interaction between discursive constructions of martial arts and the manner in which individuals conceive of and experience martial arts at the global level. Pertinent to this discussion is how commercialisation has promoted martial arts at the global arena while seemingly robbing martial arts of its "authenticity."

In Chap. 4, I illustrated how lived spaces (Lefebvre 2002) are constructed through social interactions and through how individuals utilise their bodies and senses. The lived spaces are indicative of the civilising and sportisation processes that confer upon the act of doing martial arts a sense of liminality. Shifting my analytical lens from the phenomenological study of martial arts, I shall now elucidate, vis-à-vis the processes of globalisation, how martial arts are embedded within transnational flows and practices that simultaneously feed back into the embodied and discursive construction of martial arts. Globalisation, what it encapsulates, and what consequences it has for other social institutions have been the subject of numerous academic debates (see Donnelly 1996; Friedman 1994; Grossberg 1997;

© The Editor(s) (if applicable) and The Author(s) 2016
Loh H.L.L, *The Body and Senses in Martial Culture*,
DOI 10.1057/978-1-137-55742-1_5

Magdalinski 2009; Maguire 1999, 2000; Miller et al. 2001; Ritzer 2004, 2006). In this book, I focus on aspects of transnational flows that impact the transmission and modification of sensorial knowledge and the commercialisation of martial arts. I will succinctly summarise the history of sport and its relationship to globalisation before discussing some of the implications for the development of martial arts.

Giulianotti and Robertson (2007, 1) argue that sport "in its dual role as a long-term motor and metric of transnational change" provides a distinctive lens through which to analyse the forces of globalisation. For example, sports historians analysing the linkages between sports and globalisation have shown how the globalisation of sports is implicated in the colonial project. Sports such as cricket and football have been used as a medium to "civilise" indigenous people (Guttmann 1995; Mangan 1987) and both indigenous and non-indigenous sports have been subjected to the processes of adaptation, change, and commercialisation (cf. Appadurai 1996; Giulianotti 1999). In today's milieu, sports have become institutions that are economically prominent, popular, and are able to unite and mobilise individual sentiments regardless of people's cultural differences (Eco 1987; Smart 2007). The rise of sport as an institution in the global arena is the result of commercial interests (Aris 1990; Harvey and Houle 1994; Houlihan 1994; Grant 2006; Klein 2001; Miller et al 2001; Smart 2005, 2007), multinational media corporations investing in sports, the institutionalisation of inaugural international sporting events, and the rise of governing bodies (Maguire 1999) that have sought to standardise and institutionalise sporting rules and regulations (Van Bottenburg 2001). The institutionalisation of sports results in the transnational movement and migration of sports personnel, the use of the media to deliver sporting events on a global scale, the flow of sports finances and ideas about sports across the globe, the emergence of transnational regulatory bodies and organisations for sports, and new ways in which sports are interpreted and consumed by diverse cultures (Grant 2006). However, to polarise this "global–local nexus" is unnecessarily to attribute hegemony to one pole and exclude the other (Andrews and Ritzer 2007). Robertson (1995) argues for the need to recognise the interpenetrative and complementary relations linking this nexus since the local is complicit in the creation and perpetuation of the global, and vice versa. In making its presence felt in the global arena, the institution of sport is simultaneously furthering globalisation processes in areas such as politics, culture, and the economy (see Friedman 1994; Grant 2006; Maguire 1999).

Utilising my informants' vignettes, I will elucidate the ways in which these bidirectional global flows of ethnoscapes, mediascapes, technoscapes, financescapes, and ideoscapes (Appadurai 1996, 33) impact martial arts, paying particular attention to the relationship between techniques of the body and the commercialisation of martial arts. I appropriate Appadurai's concept of "-scapes" and offer the term "martialscape" to describe the dynamic interaction between discursive constructions of martial arts and the manner in which individuals conceive of and experience martial arts at the global level. Divorcing himself from a paradigm that seeks to comprehend globalisation "in terms of existing centre-periphery models" (1990, 32), Apparadurai (1990, 295) argues that "at least as rapidly as forces from various metropolises are brought into new societies they tend to be indigenised in one or other way." Apparadurai's concept of "-scapes" is reflective of a de-territorialised, postmodern, and transnational milieu where myriad centres are involved in bidirectional processes of hybridisation that calls into question an "authentic and original" culture. Similarly, martial arts traditions, having circumvented the globe, have been transformed into de-territorialised cultural practices.

The term 'martialscape' reflects these de-territorialised cultural practices, the hybridisation process these cultural forms undergo by a receiving audience, and the transnational movement of fighters. In this chapter, I argue that the men's sojourns in Thailand are reflective of the growing popularity and commercialisation of Muay Thai and the way Muay Thai is discursively constructed as a martial art. In the preceding chapters, I showed how Muay Thai involves an embodied socialisation process that contests the men's normative ideas regarding Muay Thai and how they have already been socialised by their own cultures into using particular techniques of the body. These men are not only negotiating new ways to use their bodies but also new ways of thinking of and about their bodies. Their sojourns at *Kwaan-saa-maat Gym* highlight how ideas of Muay Thai, propelled by the sportisation process and commercial interests, circulate around the world and correspondingly impact the practice of Muay Thai in Thailand.

Sigurd   I guess you get more confident [from learning martial arts] but I noticed that I started to travel a lot more. Last year I went to Japan, Brazil, Italy, France, Sweden and England. And this year I am going to Thailand, Vietnam, Cambodia, and after Christmas I am going back to Brazil again.

Ivar   In 1993, I started with Kendo and did that for about 1 semester
        and then Karate for about 8 years. The next couple of years I
        tried different martial arts: anything from Kempo, Jiu-jitsu and
        just stuff. In 2005, I started to do some Thai boxing. After com-
        ing back from training in Thailand, it was really hard to motivate
        me to continue with the Muay T in Sweden. There wasn't any
        good training...Then I started with Brazilian jiu-jitsu 2 years ago
        and mixed martial arts.

These two extracts epitomise how globalisation has impacted the individual's quest to learn martial arts and suggests some mechanisms in which
transnational flows can impact the discursive construction of martial arts
globally.

The spread of Muay Thai across the globe is fuelled by a variety of factors such as its prominence in popular culture. Examples include the reality television show, *The Contender Asia*, which first premiered in 2008 as
an offshoot of the American boxing reality series, *The Contender* (2005);
action movies such as *Beautiful Boxer* (2004), *Ong-Bak: Muay Thai
Warrior* (2003), and *Kickboxer* (1989); and the rise of martial arts gyms
such as Singapore's *Evolve*, that hire Thai trainers to impart Muay Thai to
foreigners. Sigurd's narrative illustrates how global flows have facilitated
the men's decision to train in Thailand:

L.L   So what started you on martial arts?
Sigurd I don't know. Probably the UFC [Ultimate Fighting
        Championships, which was founded in 1993]. I wanted to learn
        how to fight so I started with Thai boxing. And my gym, we had
        both Thai and BJJ. I started doing both and after one year, the
        gym spilt. The Thai guys wanted to open their own gym so you
        had to pay for both the Thai and the BJJ. And I got BJJ. I had
        most friends in the BJJ community so I just became BJJ.

Unsurprisingly, Sigurd cited the UFC as one of the factors that sparked
off his interest in martial arts. This is because the UFC, a multimillion-
dollar MMA promotion company based in America, is responsible not
only for the sportisation process (Elias 1971) but also for facilitating the
transnational flow of televised images that impact the discursive construction of martial arts and the lived spaces of the gym (see Kraus and Aita
2002; Mayeda and Ching 2008). Commercial interests propel the sporti-

sation process. Through measures such as institutionalising an official set of rules, fixed weight classes, and the use of protective gear, the organisers attempt to redefine MMA as a mainstream sport (Van Bottenburg and Heilbron 2006). Mainstream sports like football are legitimised partially through these structural features. Elias would argue that the transition of MMA from being perceived as a deviant activity, akin to "human cock-fighting" (Gentry 2001, 73), to a mainstream activity is due to the civilising process of which the sportisation process is but one aspect. However, while it would appear that the structural evolution of MMA is characteristic of the sportisation process, interviews with my informants suggest otherwise. At the gym, the men are actively socialising their bodies to throw off the inhibitions of the civilising process. Their liminal experiences can be attributed to how the gym's regimes are constructed in opposition to this civilising process. I draw upon Meyer et al's (1997) argument to provide an alternative explanation to account for the disparity between the structural similarities of MMA with the civilising process and why the indoctrination into MMA appears to be a decivilising rather than a civilising process.

Meyer et al. (1997, 153) theorise that the structural isomorphism of nation states and organisations is premised upon their adopting the "model of the rational and responsible actor." The adoption of this model by organisations gives rise to structural isomorphism, resulting in organisations having similar characteristics in terms of their structures, policies, and conduct towards other actors at both the local and the global stages (DiMaggio and Powell 1983). Although there exist differences in the way theorists explain societal changes, structural isomorphism and the civilising process are not mutually exclusive and both work in tandem to bring about similar outcomes in areas such as sports. Elias (2000) theorises these developments as arising from changes in the way society and human relations are organised. On the other hand, Meyer et al. (1997) view structural similarities in social institutions as the result of emerging institutions attempting to legitimise themselves by imitating successful and established ones. The latter's success can be attributed to their adherence to the civilising process. The UFC, mimicking the structural features prevalent in other sports, confers onto MMA an aura of legitimacy, allowing MMA to be recognised as a legitimate sport. Structural isomorphism, which mimics the sportisation process, also accounts for why scientific discourses that attempt to rationalise, regulate, and discipline the body are increasingly prevalent in martial arts. These scientific discourses result in some of the tensions and contradictions experienced by the fighters (see Chaps. 3 and 4). Structural isomorphism is thus partially responsible for the increasing popularity of martial arts and the shifts in the way bodies are disciplined and manipulated.

THE TRANSNATIONAL FLOW OF BODILY TECHNIQUES

Sigurd's narrative highlights how the UFC is one avenue through which individuals imbibe martial arts as a self-defence system, a form of popular culture, or even as a surreal fantasy. The UFC is one medium that disseminates televised images of MMA practitioners, who draw upon eclectic fighting styles to incorporate into their growing arsenal of techniques. These fighters are actively modifying their bodies and styles in order to excel in the ring. As individuals are concerned only about the efficacy of the techniques, this process of adaptation and hybridisation results in techniques of the body being disembedded from their original martial traditions and cultures. Previously, fighters and fighting systems were rooted within a particular culture at specific geographical sites. The current martialscape with individuals mixing and matching different fighting styles defies simplistic attempts to categorise fighters as originating from a particular culture. Paul, a professional fighter, summarises the evolution of MMA through the years:

Paul   MMA is finding the best of each martial art. Each martial art has a benefit…MMA is around for 15 years. Think about when it first started, what did it look like then? It was horrible. Even the champions from 5 years ago couldn't beat the champions of today and that is a short time man. Previously it was one style versus another. You have like Karate versus say BJJ. Now everyone does the same kind of styles, training. Everyone does boxing, wrestling, Jiu-jitsu, Muay Thai so everyone knows the same basic knowledge. Now [it] is about who is [in] better shape, better conditioning, and mixing and matching.

This extract highlights how the previous era in MMA history is one where individuals are identified by their fighting styles. Implicit in this categorisation is the assumption that fighting systems can be essentialised to particular cultures and nationalities. For example, Karate fighters are often assumed to be Orientals (see Hughes 2008). Due to the free market and capitalist organisations, global sport is de-territorialised, "making it more problematic for people to identify with it as an expression of their nation" (Hargreaves 2002, 34). In a global martialscape, with fighters of different nationalities competing and being exposed to different martial bodies and fighting systems, "mixing and matching" is thus an adaptive response. Fighters, whose bodies have already been socialised into utilising particular bodily techniques, are now faced with the challenge of incorporating new bodily techniques in order to be successful in this new environment. However, as the extract below demonstrates, embodied techniques, reflective of arduous training, are not so easily forgotten:

Jack   You have an excellent sense of stability and balance.
L.L   What do you mean?
Jack   Like the other day when I was grabbing your leg after you threw the roundhouse, you were still rather stable. I guess it must be your Aikido training? So how do you find Muay Thai?
L.L   Well, it is rather difficult. Like I am not sure how to stand. It is totally different from Aikido and the ajarns keep correcting my footwork.
Jack   I used to do kickboxing and I took some time to get used to standing in the Muay Thai stance. Guess I am too used to the kickboxing stance. My stance is more like MMA than Muay Thai. I guess you have to discover it for yourself and take time to discover what works for you.

This process of "mixing and matching" is reflective of a layering of body memory as fighters attempt to find the best combination of bodily postures, movements, and techniques that suits them the best. For them, this process takes place not only at the gym but also throughout the rest of their fighting careers as they encounter new bodily techniques or learn to adapt their aging bodies to the rigours of being a fighter.

Extending my argument about how somatic culture involves a reconfiguration of the body and the senses, the "mixing and matching" of bodily techniques unifies spatial and temporal distances. In this global circuit, transnationally mobile individuals come to embody particular bodily schemata and dispositions, which they then transmit to other bodies through training or the act of dominating their competitors. Fighters like Paul, Ivar, and Sigurd, who travel to places like Thailand and Brazil to hone their technical corpus in Muay Thai and BJJ, respectively, are quite common. Spencer (2012, 98) argues that "the inscription of strategy on the bodies of fighters involves the training of specific body techniques for a future opponent, and in doing so, the fighter's body unites the past, present, and the future" in terms of bodily techniques. The fighter's body transcends not only temporal but also geographical boundaries as fighters, professional or otherwise, travel the global martial arts circuit to refine their skills and compete. There is a constant circulation of individuals, ideas, and fighting styles as individuals travel across geographical boundaries to train, test, and reaffirm their mastery of their bodies. This is exemplified in the series of MMA tournaments held in Asia, *One Fighting Championships*, where fighters from diverse countries like South Africa, Denmark, Taiwan, South Korea, Japan, and the Netherlands were brought in to draw the crowds (Lim 2011; Manila Bulletin 2011; Today 2011). The *One Fighting Championships*, an arena where fighters of diverse fighting styles have the opportunity to assert their bodily capital, testifies to the transnational and commercial nature of martial arts. For example, Paul was telling me about his plans to compete in two competitions held in the Middle East because of the comparatively more attractive prize money. Like *The Contender Asia*, the *One Fighting Championships* is indicative of how America has influenced Asia, transforming the martialscape via the flow of ideas and money. In addition, as their careers decline, some professional fighters may decide to set up martial arts gyms to impart the somatic knowledge they have gained from travelling and competing. The heightened somatic knowledge that differentiates these individuals makes them all too painfully aware of their bodily limits, which sooner or later will restrict their professional careers as fighters (see Spencer 2012) and force them to seek alternative employment such as being instructors who continue to pass on bodily techniques.

At the institutional level of MMA, this "mixing and matching" of bodily/cultural techniques is subsumed within the larger discourse of effectiveness and efficiency. Promoters for MMA fighters often emphasise how deadly the fighters are, downplay the cultural components embodied in their arsenals of bodily techniques. The men also appropriate these narratives when they analyse professional matches or their own sparring experiences. For example, in describing his first sparring match at the gym, Jack ignored how his opponent draws upon an eclectic array of martial traditions and focused on how "wicked the techniques are" and "you can really feel that punch whacking all the way into you! Bam!" For the men, what is more important is not the particular cultural origins of martial traditions but the way in which they effectively appropriate different bodily techniques. The effectiveness of bodily techniques is highly valued in this culture that prizes the experiential element above all. These discourses are thus reflective of the de-territorialisation of cultural practices epitiomised in Apparadurai's idea of "-scapes." They are also revealing of the processes of meaning-making undertaken by the men in their dual role as fighters and as the audience for others' performances in the ring.

MARTIALSCAPES AND COMMERCIALISATION

Inevitably, individuals bemoan how commercialisation has negatively impacted martial arts. Professional fighters or martial arts purists are concerned about the quality of education that is imparted by teachers of questionable credentials. Rage, 26, an American professional fighter, expressed his disgust at how commercialised the American martial arts scene is, where individuals with little or no fighting experience attempt to make a "quick buck." The disdain displayed by the men towards individuals who have questionable bodily capital reaffirms their identity as knowledgeable fighters, who have the ability to discern and confer legitimacy onto other bodies. This ability is the result of the time and effort the men have invested in cultivating their own bodies. Kenneth elaborates:

Kenneth	But finding a good instructor in America is very hard. You go to all those schools in America, it's like 5 m tall trophies. Everybody is a world champion. That is what turned me off when I was in high school. I wanted to learn Taekwondo,'cause I did it when I was a kid. I walked in and asked how much it will cost me. This guy goes, "We will put you in the black belt course. You will get your black belt in 2 years. You pay $2000 upfront."
Sigurd	Like those 2-hour Taekwondo black belts! [Laughs]
L.L	What are those?
Sigurd	You know those videos? Where they guarantee that you will be a black belt after watching their two-hour video! Instant black belt! The only faster way is if you dye the belt black yourself! [Laughs]

Another recurrent theme is that commercialisation has resulted in individuals not being socialised into learning values such as respect. The extract below suggests that this may be due to clashes between different cultural norms and values in an increasingly globalised martialscape.

Paul   I love Jiu-Jitsu but I saw a lot of things in Jiu-Jitsu I don't want my kids to experience. I think Jiu-Jitsu is a bit too cavalier? At least in America.

L.L   Cavalier as in?

Paul   Guys used to bring girls home or to the gym and do them on the mats. They thought it was funny. I never thought it was funny. You would never find these characters in judo club!

Me   That's rather disrespectful…

Paul   Like I said it is because Brazilians have a different culture and when they came to America, they brought those habits to America. Maybe it is okay in Brazil… When the Brazilians brought BJJ to America, they weren't so much about martial arts as fighting. Some of these other clubs, it is about fighting, about fighting.

The men often evoke a nostalgic martialscape, one that is untainted by commercial interests, to justify their discontent with the pedagogy of contemporary martial arts. Nostalgia, the selective reconstruction of an imagined utopian past (Chua 1995) becomes the yardstick the men use to critique contemporary martial arts. Within this martialscape, the men appear to be on a quest for "authenticity." In his conceptualisation of "-scapes," Apparadurai (1990, 31) argues that imagination is fundamental to "all forms of agency, is itself a social fact, and is the key component of the new global order" (1990, 31), resulting in individuals living "imagined worlds" (1990, 222). In this fluid and disjunctive present, authenticity is revealed to be an impossibly contradictory idea that conflates and interweaves conventional social dimensions such as class or geography with people's dreams and imaginations (Beck 2000). When the men engage in meaning and sense making as they "mix and match," not only is the "truly authentic" lost but the notion of "authenticity" is also rendered marginal. Due to the conflation of two different types of "authenticity" operating at the gym, this quest for the "authentic" is extremely complicated. In choosing Kwaan-saa-maat Gym, a gym located in the provinces, the men reaffirm their quest to experience the monastic lifestyle of a fighter by subjecting their bodies to the Spartan discipline of "traditional fighters." This quest to experience the "authentic" lifestyle of a fighter is something that the men crave. However, I previously illustrated how the "authenticity" of cultural techniques is not as important as their effectiveness in inflicting pain on their opponents. At the gym, authority is indexed against one's prowess as a fighter. The latter illustrates how contestations over "authenticity" are the "province of authority" (Fees 1996, 122), that "authenticity" is an ascribed quality and that what is recognised as "authenticity" is fluid (see Bruner 1994, 2008; Fees 1996). Friedman (1992) also critically deconstructs the notion of "authenticity" by questioning the validity of an "objective" past. Through the men's narratives, I have demonstrated how the men may buy into particular constructions of authenticity and construct a particular identity as fighters around it.

Unsurprisingly, the assumption that the transmission of martial arts was always coupled with the inculcation of particular values fails to consider how these current discourses may not be historically valid and that the "past" is discursively constructed (see Donohue 1994a, b). Furthermore, the irony is that without the globalisation of sport, it is unlikely that these individuals would have initially taken up a non-native fighting system, or positioned themselves as stakeholders in the evolution of contemporary martial arts. This is a point that David implicitly acknowledges. Although he is aware of the negative ramifications that commercialisation could potentially have for martial arts, David recognises that his ability to "put bread on the table" is the product of commercialisation, since "MMA is where the money is. You know more money is coming that way, it's growing and overtaking Muay Thai and it's in the ring." This statement reflects how the commercialisation of sports allows individuals to take up fighting as a professional career and is responsible for the current widespread popularity of martial arts.

In this chapter, I illustrate how the rise of the contemporary martialscape, embedded within global flows, is due to various factors such as structural isomorphism and capitalism. In this global martial circuit, as fighters strive for supremacy, there has been a diffusion and adaptation of bodily techniques across different cultures. One caveat is that this mixing and matching is not a laissez-faire process because of the rules and regulations that characterise the sportisation process. As capitalist institutions heavily influence this martialscape, I elucidate the tensions that arise between the opportunism that commercialisation of the sport promotes and ideas of "authenticity," and suggest that these struggles are reflective of attempts by individuals to be recognised as having the necessary and legitimate bodily capital to be a fighter. In my final chapter, I continue this discussion of transnational flows by analysing what these men got out of their sojourn at Kwaan-saa-maat Gym and how the acquisition of bodily capital from the gym has impacted their everyday life back home.

REFERENCES

Andrews, D. L., & Ritzer, G. (2007). The grobal in the sporting glocal. In R. Giulianotti & R. Robertson (Eds.), *Globalisation and sport*. Oxford: Blackwell.

Apparadurai, A. 1990. Disjuncture and Difference in the global cultural economy in Public Culture, Vol 2:2, Spring.

Appadurai, A. (1996). *Modernity at large: Cultural dimensions of globalisation*. Minneapolis: University of Minnesota Press.

Aris, S. (1990). *Sportsbiz: Inside the sports business*. London: Hutchinson.

Beck, U. (2000). What is globalisation? In J. Beynon & D. Dunkerley (Eds.), *Globalisation: The reader*. London: The Athlone Press.

Bruner, E. M. (1994). Abraham Lincoln as authentic reproduction: A critique of postmodernism. *American Anthropologist, New Series, 96*(2), 397–415.

Bruner, E. M. (2008). Lincoln's New Salem as a contested site. *Museum Anthropology, 17*(3), 14–24.

Chua, B. H. (1995). That imagined space: Nostalgia for Kampungs. In B. Yeoh & L. Kong (Eds.), *Portraits of places: History, community and identity in Singapore*. Singapore: Times Edition.

DiMaggio, P. J., & Powell, W. W. (1983). The iron cage revisited: Institutional isomorphism and collective rationality in organizational fields. *American Sociological Review, 48*(1), 147–160.

Donnelly, P. (1996). The local and the global: Globalisation in the sociology of sport. *Journal of Sport and Social Issues, 20*(1), 239–257.

Donohue, J. J. (1994a). *The martial arts and the American imagination*. West Port, CT: Bergin and Garvey.

Donohue, J. J. (1994b). *Warrior dreams: The martial arts and the American imagination*. West Port, CT: Bergin and Garvey.

Eco, U. (1987). *Travels in hyper-reality*. London: Picador.

Elias, N. (1971). The genesis of sport as a sociological problem. In E. Dunning (Ed.), *The sociology of sport: A selection of readings*. London: Frank Cass.

Elias, N. (2000). The civilising process. In: E. Dunning, J. Goudsblom, & S. Mennell (Eds.), *Sociogenetic and psychogenetic investigations* (E. Jephcott, Trans.). Cornwall: Blackwell.

Fees, C. (1996). Tourism and politics of authenticity in a North Cotswold town. In T. Selwyn (Ed.), *The tourist image: Myth and myth making in tourism*. Chichester: Wiley.

Friedman, J. (1992). The past in the future: History and the politics of identity. *American Anthropologist, 94*(4), 837–859.

Friedman, J. (1994). *Cultural identity and global process.* London: Sage Publications.

Gentry, C. (2001). *No holds barred: Evolution.* Richardson, TX: Archon.

Giulianotti, R. (1999). *Football: A sociology of the global game.* Cambridge: Polity Press.

Giulianotti, R., & Robertson, R. (2007). Sport and globalisation: Transnational dimensions. In R. Giulianotti & R. Robertson (Eds.), *Globalisation and sport.* Oxford: Blackwell.

Grant, J. (2006). *Sports, culture and society. An introduction.* London and New York: Routledge.

Grossberg, L. (1997). Cultural studies, modern logics, and theories of globalisation. In A. McRobbie (Ed.), *Back to reality? Social experience and cultural studies.* Manchester: Manchester University Press.

Guttmann, A. (1995). *Games and empires.* New York: Columbia University Press.

Hargreaves, J. (2002). Globalisation theory, global sport, and nations and nationalism. In J. Sugden & A. Tomlinson (Eds.), *Power games. A critical sociology of sport.* London and New York: Routledge.

Harvey, J., & Houle, F. (1994). Sport, world economy, global culture, and new social movements. *Sociology of Sports Journal, 11*(4), 337–355.

Houlihan, B. (1994). *Sport and international politics.* Hemel Hempstead: Harvester Wheatsheaf.

Hughes, M. (2008). *Made in America. the most dominant champion in UFC history.* New York: Simon Spotlight Entertainment.

Klein, N. (2001). *No logo.* London: Flamingo.

Kraus, E., & Aita, B. (2002). *Brawl: A behind the scenes look at mixed martial arts competition.* Toronto, Canada: ECW Press.

Lefebvre, H. (2002). The production of space. In J. D. Michael & F. Steven (Eds.), *The spaces of postmodernity. Readings in human geography.* Massachusetts, USA: Blackwell.

Lim, S. (2011, August 27). Jetsetting with Chatri Sityodtong. *Today.* Singapore: Mediacorp Press Ltd.

Magdalinski, T. (2009). *Sport, technology and the body. The nature of performance.* Abingdon: Routledge.

Maguire, J. (1999). *Global sport: Identities, societies, civilisations.* Cambridge: Polity.

Maguire, J. (2000). Sport and globalisation. In J. Coakley & E. Dunning (Eds.), *Handbook of sports studies.* London: Sage.

Mangan, J. A. (1987). *The games ethic and imperialism.* London: Viking.

Manila Bulletin. (2011, July 22). 2 Filipino URCC champions featured in biggest MMA Event in Asia. *Manila Bulletin.* Philippines: Manila Bulletin Publishing Corp.

Mayeda, D. T., & Ching, D. E. (2008). *Fighting for acceptance: Mixed martial arts and violence in American society.* New York: iUniverse.

Meyer, J. W., Boli, J., Thomas, G. M., & Ramirez, F. O. (1997). World society and the nation-state. *American Journal of Sociology, 193*(1), 144–181.

Miller, T., Lawrence, G., McKay, J., & Rowe, D. (2001). *Globalisation and sport: Playing the world.* London: Sage.

Ritzer, G. (2004). *The globalisation of nothing.* Thousand Oaks, CA: Pine Forge Press.

Ritzer, G. (2006). *McDonaldisation the reader* (2nd ed.). Thousand Oaks, CA: Pine Forge Press.

Robertson, R. (1995). Glocalisation: Time-space and homogeneity-heterogeneity. In M. Featherstone, S. Lash, & R. Robertson (Eds.), *Global modernities.* London: Sage.

Smart, B. (2005). *The sport star: Modern sport and the making of modern sport.* London: Allen Lane.

Smart, B. (2007). Not playing around: Global capitalism, modern sport and consumer culture. In R. Giulianotti & R. Robertson (Eds.), *Globalisation and sport.* Oxford: Blackwell.

Spencer, D. C. (2012). *Ultimate fighting and embodiment. Violence, gender, and mixed martial arts.* New York: Routledge.

Today. (2011, September 3). SportsZone ventures into the fighting cage. *Today.* Singapore: Mediacorp Press Ltd.

Van Bottenburg, M. (2001). *Global games.* Urbana: University of Illinois Press.

Van Bottenburg, M., & Heilbron, J. (2006). De-sportization of fighting contests: The origins and dynamics of no holds barred events and the theory of sportization. *International Review for the Sociology of Sports, 41*(3), 259–282.

CHAPTER 6

Conclusion

Abstract In the concluding chapter of this book, I analyse what these men got out of their sojourn at *Kwaan-saa-maat Gym*. For some, their total immersion in this somatic culture stops upon leaving the gym, while for others, somatic, masculine culture has transformed their outlook on life and their bodily dispositions. They shared that the acquisition of bodily capital from the gym has impacted their everyday life back home as the transformation of their physique, coupled with the knowledge that is embodied within them, results in their carrying themselves better, having a better posture and a keener ability to discern changes in their immediate surroundings.

In the preceding chapters, I described the gym's everyday rhythms and how the fighters' masculine ethos is both discursively and somatically sustained via a series of performances and social interactions. To be a fighter, one needs to be socialised into a masculine, somatic culture. This entails embodying foreign bodily techniques and putting aside inhibitions pertaining to the usage of violence. I first historically situated the latter via Elias's (2000) "civilising process" before drawing upon Lefebvre's (2002) conceptual triad of space to theorise how the sensorium is an avenue by which martial disciplines become embodied. The centrality of the body in unifying these chapters highlights the limitations of adhering to Descartes's mind–body dualism. Power permeates the gym and there exists a hierarchical order of bodies and masculinities. Certain bodies, which possess the correct bodily capital, have the ability to be self-authorising and command the respect of others. Consequently, the men often attempt to replicate or mould their bodies into the ideal type or risk being subjugated or marginalised.

Beneath this veneer of camaraderie, there is then a darker side to the gym. I illuminated the inherent contradictions encapsulated within the fighter's ethos as I described the fighters' routines and regimes and their acquisition of particular bodily frames of behaviour and somatic knowledge. I argue that the men engaged in body projects (Shilling 1993) that simultaneously embody rationality and irrationality. This "irrationality" is manifested as either an excessive emotional obsession with martial arts or prematurely damaging the body. For the latter, they subject their bodies to harsh physical regimes that promise optimal physical performance in return for a shortened fighting career due to the onset of injuries and age (see Chap. 4). In addition, they constantly normalise their participation in this somatic culture, labelled by outsiders as physical, violent, brutal, and at odds with the everyday norms, by rationalising their actions through scientific discourses, framing martial arts as a mentally engaging activity, or highlighting that the sacrifices and opportunity costs made in return for the invaluable lessons on life and bodily capital were worth it. Yet, this rationality is relative because there exists a moral dimension to the men's actions as well. Although the men's participation in this somatic culture may appear to be irrational to outsiders, for them, it is irrational not to conform to the gym's social norms and regulate their bodies and diet. Men who fail to conform will be subjected to the discourse on obesity with its moral dimensions of how obese individuals are decadent (e.g., Evans 2006; Hoverd and Sibley 2007; Moulding 2003; Saguy and Gruys 2010; Saguy and Almeling 2008). Similarly, analysis of other body projects such as plastic surgery (Atkinson 2008; Blum 2003; Davis 2008) and bodybuilding (Brown and Graham 2008; Crossley 2006; Fussell 1991; Gill et al. 2005; Rosen 1983) uncover this tension between emic and etic definitions of rationality where societal definitions of what constitute rationality often take on a radically different meaning within the confines of particular somatic cultures.

The malleability of the body thus translates to individuals having the "means to exert an unprecedented degree of control over bodies," yet having radical doubt about the "knowledge of what bodies are and how we should control them" (Shilling 1993, 3). At the gym, rationality is layered because different perspectives are brought to bear, resulting in the men appearing to oscillate between rationality/irrationality. Drawing on these narratives, I contest current approaches of analysing somatic cultures through the framework either of rational body projects or of affect because elements of both are clearly present. Individuals are not always rational, and often operate outside the normative boundaries of what is perceived to be logical. Somatically, this oscillation between rationality and irrationality arises from the body "failing" to live up to the "rational" demands placed upon it and breaking down in the face of physical duress. The body often evades the best attempts to regulate, discipline, and control it. The embodiment of particular bodily frames of reference/techniques of the body, from prior socialisation, often surfaces unexpectedly, in defiance of what the individual demands of his body. The men most acutely experience this when they attempt to learn Muay Thai and have to either put aside or mix and match the various martial disciplines already embodied within their beings.

Informed by Nancy (2000, 2008), I address the ocularcentrism prevalent in previous phenomenological works. I examined bodily frames of reference, paying attention to how being a fighter requires not only a repository of techniques but also intimate somatic awareness. The men often comment that language is not a barrier to learning Muay Thai because "some things can be learned through observations" (Michael) and that "pantomiming is a universal language" (Aaron). However, the fact that the men expressed the non-ocularcentric aspects of Muay Thai only after intensive probing testifies to the prevalence of ocularcentrism and the difficulty in conveying somatic knowledge verbally. This is due to the historical occlusion of the senses other than that of sight and the recent "rediscovery" of the other senses in the twentieth century (Jutte 2005). Muay Thai therefore requires particular techniques of the body (Mauss 2006[1934]), aside from simply observing, and an aesthetic that needs to be inculcated. Rather than continue to perpetuate a hierarchy of the senses or analyse each sense in isolation, I argue for the need to analyse the senses holistically, and to pay attention to how the sensorium impacts not only cultural transmission but also identity formation (e.g., Hockey 2006).

This phenomenological element and the men's constant rationalisation of their participation in this somatic culture are recurrent themes. Featherstone (1992) examines the dichotomy between the "everyday life" and the "heroic life." Here, I focus on aspects of the everyday and the heroic, as he defines them, that have immediate ramifications in the context of my research. For Featherstone (1992, 160–161), the everyday is demarcated by "an emphasis upon what happens every day, the routine, repetitive taken-for-granted experiences, beliefs and practices" and concerns "the sphere of reproduction and maintenance, a pre-institutional zone in which the basic activities which sustain other worlds are performed." In contrast, the heroic life refers to the quest for excitement, subjecting the self to peril and requiring the necessary courage to depart from the mundane. For these men who have fled their everyday routines at home, their sojourn in a foreign martial arts gym and learning to throw aside the inhibitions of the "civilising process" (Elias 2000), is a liminal experience. This liminality is both phenomenological and structural. The investments they made in order to partake in the heroic life translate into greater somatic awareness, the indoctrination of particular bodily techniques and sensory dispositions, assuming the identity of a masculine fighter, the possession of bodily capital, and a leaner physique. To belong to this somatic culture, one must not only share the same worldview, beliefs, and practices but must also be able to convey to others during non-verbal sparring sessions that they have acquired the desired bodily capital and sensory knowledge.

The men's presence at the gym reflects how globalisation and commercialisation has resulted in the deterritorialisation of global sports and the "mixing and matching" of various disciplines as they attempt to find the most efficient and effective combination. These men value practicality and efficacy over other considerations such as martial traditions. However, they too comment about how martial arts have taught them discipline and focus (see Chap. 3 and Appendix A). Given that these men are embedded within global flows, I shall now briefly discuss what the men do with the bodily capital that they gained in exchange for monetary capital upon returning home. As the men continue to travel across different martialscapes to learn, teach, or compete, these somatic experiences come to be constituted within larger transnational flows of bodily dispositions and knowledge. For others, their quest to be fighters stops when they leave the gym. However, their immersion in this somatic, masculine culture has transformed their outlook on life and their bodily dispositions. The men's investment in this "heroic life" consequently impacts the way they view "the everyday." In general, the men become more confident. For example, Kelvin says,

> I wouldn't go around trying to get into a fight now but I know that if anything happens, I can defend myself. There is this confidence that I can do it.

Some men also comment on how the transformation of their physique, coupled with the knowledge that is embodied within them, results in their carrying themselves better, having a better posture, and a keener ability to discern changes in their immediate surroundings. After leaving the field, I continue to interact with the men through Facebook. Many still express their desire to return to the gym, nostalgically remembered as a period where "life is good. No need to worry about work, bringing home the bacon. You just wake up, train, and sleep. You can be focused on just training" (Rage). They talk about saving money for another trip back to the gym. Despite the gym being constructed as a liminal space, divorced from the rhythms of everyday capitalism, monetary considerations will always intrude upon this martial space.

In conclusion, this ethnographic study of a martial arts gym in Thailand elucidates how culture impacts bodily dispositions and the way one thinks about and through the body. As a martial artist myself, I provided an ethnographic account of the lives of fighters. The use of an embodied methodology sensitised me to the non-verbal somatic interactions that constitute one of the fundamental pillars of the gym's culture. I highlighted the benefits of analysing how somatic knowledge mediates the transmission of culture, paying attention to how sensory dispositions impact one's social interactions and ontological perceptions about the world. I then demonstrated how the sensorium is an important avenue to analyse culture and how macro forces such as globalisation have modified and transformed existing cultural practices. My research has demonstrated the need to think holistically about the sensorium vis-à-vis somatic practices and cultures, and to transcend the rationality/irrationality dichotomy prevalent in works dealing with the body and the senses.

REFERENCES

Atkinson, M. (2008). Exploring male femininity in the 'crisis': Men and cosmetic surgery. *Body and Society, 14*(1), 67–97.

Blum, V. L. (2003). *Flesh wounds. The culture of cosmetic surgery.* Los Angeles: University of California Press.

Brown, J., & Graham, D. (2008). Body satisfaction in gym-active males: An exploration of sexuality, gender and narcissism. *Sex Roles, 59*(1–2), 94–106.

Crossley, N. (2006). In the gym motives, meanings and moral careers. *Body and Society, 12*(3), 25–50.

Davis, K. (2008)[1995]. *Reshaping the female body. The dilemma of cosmetic surgery.* New York and London: Routledge.

Elias, N. (2000). The civilising process. In: E. Dunning, J. Goudsblom, & S. Mennell (Eds.), *Sociogenetic and psychogentic investigations* (E. Jephcott, Trans.). Cornwall: Blackwell.

Evans, B. (2006). 'Gluttony or sloth': Critical geographies of bodies and morality in (Anti)obesity policy. *Area, 38*(3), 259–267.

Featherstone, M. (1992). The heroic life and everyday life. *Theory, Culture and Society, 9*(1), 159–182.

Fussell, S. (1991). *Muscle: Confessions of an unlikely body builder.* New York: Poseidon Press.

Gill, R., Henwood, K., & McLean, C. (2005). Body projects and the regulation of normative masculinity. *Body and Society, 11*(1), 37–62.

Hockey, J. (2006). Sensing the run: The senses and distance running. *Senses and Society, 1*(2), 183–202.

Hoverd, J. W., & Sibley, C. G. (2007). Immoral bodies: The implicit association between moral discourse and the body. *Journal for the Scientific Study of Religion, 46*(3), 391–403.

Jutte, R. (2005). *A history of the senses. From antiquity to cyberspace.* Cambridge: Polity Press.

Lefebvre, H. (2002). The production of space. In J. D. Michael & F. Steven (Eds.), *The spaces of postmodernity. Readings in human geography.* Massachusetts, USA: Blackwell.

Mauss, M. (2006)[1935]. Techniques of the body. In: N. Schlanger (Ed., Introduced) *Techniques, technology and civilisation.* New York: Durkheim Press.

Moulding, N. (2003). Constructing the self in mental health practice: Identity, individualism and the feminisation of deficiency. *Feminist Review, 75*(1), 57–74.

Nancy, J. L. (2000). *Being singular plural.* Stanford, CA: Stanford University Press.

Nancy, J. L. (2008). *Corpus.* New York: Fordham University Press.

Rosen, T. (1983). *Strong and sexy: The new body beautiful.* London: Columbus Books.

Saguy, A. C., & Almeling, R. (2008). Fat in the fire? Science, the news media, and the 'obesity epidemic'. *Sociological Forum, 23*(1), 53–83.

Saguy, A. C., & Gruys, K. (2010). Morality and health: News media constructions of overweight and eating disorders. *Social Problems, 57*(2), 231–250.

Shilling, C. (1993). *The body and social theory.* London, Newbury Park: Sage.

APPENDIX A: INFORMANTS' BIOGRAPHIES

This section provides brief narratives of the biographies, motivations, and experiences of the men as they embark on their quest to acquire knowledge of martial arts. The recurrent themes of these narratives mirror the issues addressed in my thesis.

Aaron is a 27-year-old American undergraduate. He is currently on a 1-year exchange programme at a Thailand university. He is not new to *Kwaan-saa-maat Gym*, having trained there the previous year. He is quite frank about his motivations behind enrolling in an exchange programme in Thailand. He says that although the Thailand university that he is currently enrolled in is "not the best university for political science [since] it is not too connected to the American political system which I am supposed to be studying, at least I can learn Muay Thai. I want to come out here just so that I can be in Thailand and continue fighting." Interestingly, his choice of academic electives is also influenced by whether they clash with his training sessions. He views this sojourn as an opportunity to compete professionally and if he is successful, he plans to continue to stay in Thailand to train and compete. Thailand is perceived by him to be the place to go if one wants to get quality, high-intensity training.

At the age of 14, Aaron started learning Brazilian Jiu Jitsu but has since moved on to Muay Thai because of its "deep cultural meaning." He says that "the traditions that they [Muay Thai fighters] did a hundred years ago is still being practiced today. People still do the *Wai Khru*, pay respects, and sip water from the other coach after the fight." In addition, the appeal

© The Editor(s) (if applicable) and The Author(s) 2016
Loh H.L.L, *The Body and Senses in Martial Culture*,
DOI 10.1057/978-1-137-55742-1

of fighting for Aaron is that it is an "empowering experience. It gives you confidence" as he learns not to be afraid of being punched.

Reflexively, Aaron feels that the training in Muay Thai has improved his mental focus and fortitude. He says, "I don't think in the ring. Especially in my fight, I get in there and you don't think of anything man. You just think of how I want to hit this guy and I don't want to get hit and that's it. You don't think of your bills, you don't think of your girlfriend, you don't think of anything else other than just the moment." Physically, Aaron says he has lost 30 pounds within the last 2 years. His leaner physique has given him greater self-confidence and he carries himself better. For him, "Muay Thai gives you goals and something that you can aspire to."

After his short stay at Kwaan-saa-maat Gym, Aaron has been busy juggling both Muay Thai and his academic electives.

Alvin is a 22-year-old Dane. He is currently unemployed. He heard about Kwaan-saa-maat Gym from his friends and decided to come here to train for two weeks. He hopes that the training will help prepare him for his upcoming shoot fight. A shoot fight is at a level below an amateur fight and takes place at the gym. Despite being relatively new to the world of martial arts, Alvin is very passionate about martial arts. He started learning MMA only six months back. He says that this passion was sparked off when he saw his friend fighting in an MMA cage. He elaborates, "When he [his friend] got up in that cage, I was like, 'I need to get on in that cage'. I felt that it could be really cool if I could fight so of course I need to get in shape. Getting into fights is what kept me doing MMA and the adrenaline really rocks!" For him, getting in shape and having faster reflexes is another useful benefit of training. His passion for MMA can also be seen in how he continues to train despite his injuries.

Although Alvin lost his shoot fight, he remains undaunted and continues to train MMA on a regular basis, five times a week.

Andrew is a 30-year-old professional fighter who owns an export business. He is from the People's Republic of China (PRC). As a professional fighter who has to watch his weight, Andrew is very health-conscious and meticulous about his dietary requirements. He is a regular at the gym, often staying for a couple of weeks each time to prepare for his upcoming fights. Before embarking on his second career as a professional fighter, he was in the special armed forces division in the PRC army.

Being transnationally mobile, Andrew continues to travel around the world to compete in professional competitions.

David is a 33-year-old Danish professional fighter who owns Kwaan-saa-maat Gym. He has an animated personality, often narrating tales of his previous matches and the colourful personalities he encountered during his past trips. He cites his brother and the movie *Kickboxer* as reasons behind him taking up Muay Thai. Despite doing Muay Thai for more than 20 years, David says that the main appeal of Muay Thai for him is the notion of "these two guys who have both trained hard for this opening event and they go in there and try to beat the shit out of each other." Recently, David has shifted from only competing in Muay Thai to competing in MMA as well. Some reasons behind this shift include the fact that "more money is coming that way [MMA], it is growing and overtaking Muay Thai" and that MMA is more "real." David explains, "I thought that Muay Thai was real. That was like the closest thing I had seen to a real fight. Muay Thai was that kind of martial arts and that was why I got into Muay Thai. It was the best of the best and what I saw that in MMA everyone was getting choked down, taken down… the greatest stand-up fighters were being choked down… I decided to make the switch. I am not into Muay Thai for the sport, realism and the fighting aspects are important too."

Looking back, David feels that martial arts have made him a more disciplined person and "keep [him] off the street" since he could not be "out every night messing up his life when [he] has things to look forward to." As a professional fighter, running and conditioning are part of David's everyday life and he looks forward to the "sparring, the training, the getting in shape, and doing all the road work that needs to be done" before any fight. However, David admits that the life of a professional fighter has taken a heavy toll on his body. "Souvenirs" from his past fights include broken jaw, bones, ribs, knees, ankles, toes, and nose. These injuries sensitise him to the possibility of ending his career of being a professional fighter in the near future. He says, "Everyone has to face that part. I am not getting any younger and with old age comes slowing down. I may be smarter than some of these guys but I know very well that conditioning and that dream in your heart make up for that. The dream in my heart may also be burning out. So when there is less of a heart, less conditioning, just trying to make a buck while you are going against someone living his dreams… He is young, fast… He may not be as gifted but he is giving 300% and even if we are both well-conditioned, he may even have an upper hand. But I love the game!"

David continues to fight professionally and has recently won a match held in Southeast Asia. In addition, he has recently established another gym outside of Thailand.

Henry is a 25-year-old Swedish professional fighter. He has been practising Muay Thai for almost 2 years and aside from David, the owner of the gym, he has stayed the longest at the gym. He decided on this gym because of David's formidable reputation within the pugilistic circle. Prior to travelling to Thailand, Henry was in the military as Sweden had compulsory military conscription then. He worked as a security guard for 3 years before deciding that he needed a change in his life because he was bored. Since he has always loved Muay Thai, he decided to "do it professionally. That has been the goal from the start." He was musing how if he was not in Thailand, training and fighting, he would most probably still be in the army.

The appeal of Muay Thai for Henry is because he feels that it is the most brutal martial art. He says that the feeling of knocking someone out is fun. He explains that there is "that fantastic feeling when you knee someone in the head and you see the eye rolling." However, far from being a simple brawler, Henry always enters the ring with a game plan in mind and strategises. To him, Muay Thai is tough both physically and mentally. Despite suffering numerous injuries such as a broken hand and knee before, he shrugs these off as "common injuries in this game." His love for Muay Thai also largely stems from the feeling of utter exhaustion that comes from having endured an intense training session.

Henry considers himself to be a professional fighter because this is where he gets his money. He says that it is not that "glamorous but I like it. I don't have a lot of money but it is still better than the secure life I had back in Sweden." Like David, he has also started to compete in MMA fights since "MMA is probably where the money is. MMA is not that big in Thailand yet so I have to go abroad to fight. It's more money." Despite the opportunity costs of staying in Thailand for more than 2 years, he feels that the sacrifices are worth it because Muay Thai is best done when he is young. Henry knows that there will come a time when he will have to retire because of age. Reflexively, Henry feels that through learning Muay Thai, he has become more confident about himself and has learnt invaluable life experiences, such as learning to be independent in a foreign country. He has put on more than 15 kilograms of muscle and his stamina has also improved tremendously.

Henry is still training intensively in Thailand and getting more fights under his belt to build up his reputation as a fighter.

Ivar is a 39-year-old Swedish security guard. The last time he was at Kwaan-saa-maat Gym was more than 5 years ago. This is his second trip to the gym. In addition to training at Kwaan-saa-maat Gym, he has also trained at other gyms in Thailand before. He values the training that he gets in Thailand because compared to Sweden, it is cheaper, the student to teacher ratio is smaller, and there is more personalised attention given to the students. Amongst all the fighters, Ivar follows a very disciplined and regimented lifestyle. He will religiously go for his morning runs and be asleep by 9 p.m. every night to prepare his body for the training next day.

His journey into the world of martial arts first started in 1993. He trained in various martial disciplines such as Kendo, Karate, Kempo, and Jiu Jitsu. Seven years back, he first started practising Muay Thai in Thailand before making a switch to Brazilian Jiu Jitsu and MMA 2 years back because in "Sweden, it was hard to motivate me to continue with Muay Thai as the training wasn't as good." The learning of these different martial disciplines reflects his quest to find the best martial arts. The intellectual aspect of martial arts, which Ivar compares to playing "three dimensional chess," is the reason behind his sustained interest. Some important lessons, which he says he learnt through practising martial arts, include learning to persevere, establishing long-term and short-term goals.

Ivar is currently back in Sweden. He has been actively training and competing in various Brazilian Jiu Jitsu tournaments. He has since had a couple of matches.

Jack is a 22-year-old Swede. He is currently unemployed. Previously working as a manager at a restaurant, Jack quit his job and decided to go to Thailand to practise Muay Thai for 2 months.

Although he can be considered relatively new to martial arts, having only started training in various disciplines like kickboxing and Sanda for about a year-and-a-half, Jack is really passionate about them. Sanda is a fighting system that has its origins in China. As a combat sport, it combines kickboxing with takedowns. He believes that each martial discipline has its own strengths, and experimenting with different disciplines is one way he can find out what is best for his body. Full-contact martial disciplines appeal to him the most because of "the adrenalin you get from not knowing what happens next. If you get smacked to the ground or... you don't know and that is the thing I like!" The unpredictability of what may happen in a fight is perceived by Jack to be a way of testing himself physically and mentally since MMA "is about the tactical stuff." Through these trials and tribulations, one can know one's strengths and weaknesses.

Although Jack says that he feels more confident about himself now, he dismisses the nature of martial arts as being the cause. Instead, he feels that his self-confidence arises from "just knowing that you are good at something. This is a very nice feeling to have." In addition, the feeling of knowing that he is constantly improving himself motivates him further. His passion for the discipline is reflected in how he believes that "you can always train. Even if you are injured you can do some kind of training. You should do some kind of training. I don't believe you cannot do any unless you are paralysed or something." In Sweden, he trains for 2 hours daily.

Jack is currently back in Sweden, working. He is saving his money so that he can embark on another training trip in the near future.

James is a 20-year-old Swede who is currently unemployed. He is heavily tattooed. A tattoo of a Muay Thai fighter doing the Ram Muay on his pectoral muscle is his most distinguishing feature. To fund his trip to Thailand, he took out a huge loan back home. He is a rather tough fighter who has a long reach and good stamina.

Karl is a 22-year-old Scot who has just completed his master's. He is taking a respite from his studies by training at the gym. His parents work in multinational corporations and, as a result, since he was young, he has travelled a lot. Since his undergraduate years, he started on boxing because it is very popular in the UK and, institutionally, there are more avenues to take up boxing there than Muay Thai. He confesses that boxing remains his greatest love. Being an amateur boxer who has fought numerous fights, the appeal for boxing lies in how "you think more with your head when you box. That's why they call it the sweet science." He feels that even if he stops competing when he reaches his thirties, he will still continue training since he "love[s] boxing. Always have, man. I think about it a lot. It is always on my mind."

Karl leads a very disciplined life. For example, he abstains from alcohol during the weekdays. If he has an upcoming fight, he will totally eliminate alcohol and junk food from his diet. This discipline also translates to the way in which he views his life. He says, "You know I have been more mature? I have grown up a lot. When people learn martial arts, it gives you violence and serenity. You understand things like violence more and it is about the competition. You don't go in fighting angry. It is not fighting although physically you are fighting but mentally it is more like playing football or rugby. It is training to reach a goal."

Karl is back in the UK doing his PhD programme and, as always, is training intensively.

Kelvin is a 28-year-old South African. He is currently working in South Korea as a pre-school teacher. He has been doing martial arts such as

Muay Thai, Jiu Jitsu, boxing, and grappling for about 5 years but admits that because of issues such as having a hectic schedule and injuries, he did not train consistently. He holds the opinion that martial arts are a way by which to "test yourself. A lot of sports are team sports where you can just rely on other people. But in martial arts, it is just one on one. You can test yourself and it makes you tougher because of the competitive element!" This competitive element that Kelvin speaks of constantly drives him to train to be better physically and mentally. Like some of the men at the gym, Kelvin has fought in a semi-professional MMA televised match and has competed in seven Jiu Jitsu competitions.

Although Kelvin comments that in these competitions "sometimes when I get my ass kicked it is not so good, but sometimes, it is really good when you and someone else is giving it his all. Like you taking a good shot, you give a good shot and you feel very alive. So it is cool to compete with someone because it is man against man. It is like a very small universe with 2 guys slugging it out and there being only one winner."

Kelvin feels that martial arts have also impacted his outlook on life. He says, "It helped me to face tough things. By knowing that I can get through training twice a day, I think I can get through personal problems as well. So it definitely has a positive impact on me. But there are negative aspects as well such as injuries and times when I doubt myself. In general, I think the impact has been positive." Physically, he feels "fitter, stronger, more powerful with better cardio. You have more confidence in yourself because you are in better shape and healthier than people who don't do anything." His prior training as a personal trainer also means that he has knowledge of the dietary requirements of a fighter and tries his best to eat healthy.

Kelvin is still teaching in South Korea.

Michael is an 18-year-old Norwegian. He has been training in Muay Thai for about a year now and has previously spent some time at another gym in Phuket. Comparing Kwaan-saa-maat Gym to the other gym he was at last year, he feels that Kwaan-saa-maat Gym is less commercialised and the men here train on a more regular basis. He attributes this to the gym's isolated location and the fact that it is not like the gyms in Phuket, which are little more than "tourist traps." He has already chalked up one professional fight in Thailand last year and is eager to have more experience fighting in the ring. Interestingly, Michael has great awareness of his body. For example, he mentioned how he is able to use body to gauge the distance that he has run.

Michael is back in Norway after travelling and visiting various gyms located in Chiang Mai and Phuket. Needless to say, he has also managed to have more fights under his belt.

Paul is a 34-year-old American professional fighter. His parents were from the Republic of China and he holds dual citizenship. Paul still travels around the world on a regular basis, competing professionally and conducting seminars in Brazilian Jiu Jitsu, a discipline that he holds a black belt in. Since he was young, Paul has done Taekwondo, and, in high school, he started wrestling. Like some of the men, televised images sparked off his initial interest in MMA. He elaborates, "Around that time in 1994 I saw a video. My brother actually showed me a video, first couple of Ultimate Fighting Championships and when I watched it, it was kind of cool." This started him on his lifelong journey in martial arts. He says, "You do more fights and before you know it, you get pot committed. [Pot committed is a phrase commonly used in poker games. It refers to a player who has invested the majority of his chips and will have little reserves left should he loses his hand. Figuratively, Paul uses this term to highlight his heavy investment in martial arts thus far such that he has no choice but to continue his investment in martial arts.] And that is how I am in Jiu Jitsu, I am pot committed and my whole adult existence is based around martial arts. At one point I was a young guy, trying to take out guys my age now. Now I learn as much as I can, train as much as I can, to prevent that 19-year-old guy from taking me out. Either way you got to be in the gym. If you try to get to the top, you better be in the gym hustling. You want to stay in the game, you better be in the gym hustling. I enjoy Jiu Jitsu and martial arts, man!"

His passion for martial arts is sustained by the fact that "every couple of months, you get to go out there and you get to determine your future." He remarks, "Do you know how many people they work 9 to 5 jobs for 30 years, they eat breakfast everyday the same time, they go to work the same time, they pick up their kid the exact same time? Life is like just a routine for them. For me, every 3 months, I get to go out and find something about myself. That's really intense man! As the fight gets closer, your body just knows. Your body knows that something is going to happen this week. With each passing day your are a bit more keen, a bit more aware of things going around you and your body just changes man! What's going to happen? Your future is undecided! That's the kind of excitement that I like! Like I said, no one knows what is going to happen. I love that feeling! No risk, no reward. I just cannot see myself like one of those guys. I used to be a high school teacher and I lived that routine. Everyday I wake up at 8 a.m. and every day I get home by 5 p.m. You know this is cool because you are making good money but after a while you are like man I am 23 years old and my life is a routine already?" Immersing himself within the martial arts culture also results in him saying that although he "initially thought it was kind of violent, it does not feel violent anymore." In addition, despite the hard life of a fighter, Paul says, "When I am actually in the ring, win, lose or draw, you are not thinking about the money, you are not thinking about fame. When you are actually in the ring, you are throwing punches, you are fighting for survival man. It is the greatest feeling there is! I think that is why you see all these boxers come back after they retire because that feeling, you cannot get it anywhere else. You think you will get it from opening a business? You think you are going to get it from getting married? Nothing I ever experienced matches that feeling!"

However, there is also a darker side of martial arts. Paul talks about the sacrifices he has made. He says, "The cost to your family life, your personal life is tremendous. I missed lots of moments. My only brother, when his daughter was born I was getting ready for a fight. I was not there when she was born… Looking back, would it have made a big difference to have missed two days of training to go see my brother's daughter? But you know man, if you want to be the CEO of a company, you want to rise to the top, you better sacrifice. If you do not want to sacrifice, be satisfied selling cigarettes at 7–11. The more you want to achieve anything, the greater the price of sacrifice." Rather than age and injuries being causes that halt his current career, Paul comments that the fact that he is now starting to think about all the "missed weddings and birthdays" may result in him retiring because he is tired and he does not want to train anymore.

Paul is currently touring Asia and the States competing and conducting martial arts seminars.

Peder is a 22-year-old Swede who is currently unemployed. Peder is the tallest guy at the gym and has a rather bulky build. However, because he does not train with the men often, does not take part in any of the sparring sessions and likes to boast about how he is going to be an UFC champion in 5 years; the men often take his words with a pinch of salt and ridicule him. Peder has a huge appetite, and he once boasted about how he had a super-sized garlic bread, pancakes, and two large pizzas for dinner. The men expressed their disdain and amazement at this act that blatantly contradicts the gym's regimented culture. Ever since he got into a fight with Alvin and lost, Peder often stays in his room and does not socialise with the men much. The consensus amongst the men was that not only did Peder not fight back after he was punched but also failed to conduct himself in a manner worthy of a fighter. In his defence, Peder argues that "[L.L] work out in Singapore but back home in Sweden my friends and I will just hang around, eat all sorts of junk food and smoke weed. For 6 years! So I need time to get used to the training and the life here!"

Peder is currently back home in Sweden hoping to fulfil his dream of being the next world champion in MMA.

Rage is a 26-year-old American professional fighter. He often expresses his disdain at how commercialised the martial arts scene in the USA is. He says that individuals of questionable credentials setting up their own martial arts schools have become the norm. In his youth, he has done quite a bit of wrestling and Muay Thai. He says, "This is why I like wrestling and Muay Thai. There are no belts. Either you are good or you are not. Again, Las Vegas, where I train, there are a lot of wrestlers. There are no belts there. Either you can wrestle or you cannot. None of this nonsense about belts and paying money for grading."

Rage is back in the USA teaching in a martial arts gym.

Ray is a 19-year-old British law undergraduate. Prior to coming to Kwaan-saa-maat Gym, he has been training at other Muay Thai gyms in Thailand for a couple of weeks. This trip to Thailand is to allow him to take a break before university officially commences. He has done Judo for a while before his close friend introduced Muay Thai to him. He likes the culture of Muay Thai, where "after the fight, there will never be bad blood, people do not badmouth each other. I also like the traditional element in Muay Thai such as the wai khru."

Ray is rather conscious about his diet and says, "I watch my diet. I just try not to eat shit. I wouldn't eat cream, sauces, cakes and shit like that everyday. I try to stick to healthy food and I try to eat as much fruits, good carbohydrates, and protein [as I can]." With regards to the effects of training, Ray says, "I have better cardio. I feel my body gotten stronger. I can take hits much better. It is everything really. I feel healthy, I feel better." However, he admits, "My knees are starting to hurt... I been training in Thailand for like one month and one week already and my body starts to break down." In addition, he also has to grapple with feelings of loneliness. He elaborates, "I would consider myself to be quite an intellectual person and I get bored rather quickly. You know I am not much of a slave to routine. So it is quite hard for me... been very tough but in a way it is rewarding because the training will pay off and you feel the improvements and you are pleased with yourself for having maintained the focus." These feelings are exacerbated when he is injured, unable to train, and find other activities to occupy his time. Commenting on the boredom, "part of it is mental and physical as well. You get the lack of mental stimulation and you got the physical effects of just exercising too much. It takes a long time to condition yourself to be able to train twice a day every day and not feel it." Furthermore, his recent shoulder injury has made him feel more melancholic. He says, "I mean if you break an arm it heals, but dislocate a shoulder it will always be a problem. Always going to be... This shoulder is always going to be with me."

Regarding his views on signing up for a fight, Ray explains, "I just want to test my skills. I don't want to go and hurt someone because at the end of the day, it is a sport. I am not doing this because I want to hurt people and I cannot find a legal way to express the feeling. I do so because I love the sport and I want to test my skills. I been training so long now that I think I need to get into the ring and just see. Right now I have been training well but I need to see if I can fight well as well."

Overall, Ray feels that because of Muay Thai, he has "become more of a focused person... Even back home, if you are prepared to get back from home or school and go straight to training, you develop a mental attitude or focus and there is not much you wouldn't do. You don't become lazy. When I was taking the 2 years course to prepare myself for the A levels, I only took up Muay Thai in the second year. During the first year, I would get back from school-I always go to sleep really late and then wake up-really tired, feeling pretty lazy, have a sleep, wake up, sort of fuck about on the computer, television, and then try to do my work from like 10 p.m. onwards. Whereas when I was doing Muay Thai, I will go to sleep early because I am tired. I wake up, feel refreshed during the day and I start to eat well, and drink a lot of water. After school, I will go straight to training and after that, instead of lounging about, I want to go to bed at 11 p.m. so I have to get started on my homework early. So you go straight home, do your work, go to sleep. Gives you more of a focus." However, Ray acknowledges that Muay Thai will not be an intimate part of his life in the future since "I think to myself I been spending five weeks doing this [Muay Thai] and nothing else. That is a long time to be committed to one thing. What might I achieve from this? Is this going to be something I am going to use? Honestly I do see myself doing this in the university. I would love to do that if I have the time. But at the end of the day, I see myself as being a professional, a lawyer, working in the bank or something like that. Honestly I don't reckon I have the time? Maybe I would be able to do a bit of the bags at the gym or do a session? But if I have children, I wouldn't want them to get involved in it. I wouldn't want to be worrying how am I going to get to Muay Thai everyday when I got a demanding high pressure job. I rather be emotionally rather than physically satisfied. At the moment, I am young and I got a lot of free time so it is a good thing to do but at the end of the day, I could never see myself coming to Thailand to train unless it is part of the university requirements, like you currently studying, but I could never see myself doing it again really."

Currently back in the UK, Ray is pursuing his law degree and training in Muay Thai whenever the time permits.

Sigurd is a 27-year-old Norwegian car mechanic. This is his first time travelling to Thailand. He decided on Thailand because he "wanted to do some stand-up fighting and Thailand is a good place to come. It is cheap and has good training!" Previously, he took up Taekwondo but has since moved on to Brazilian Jiu Jitsu and grappling. He has been training in the latter two disciplines for about 4 years now. He cites the UFCs as the main reason behind taking up MMA. However, because knockout sports are banned in Norway, he says that he has to go to Sweden, England, or Demark if he wishes to have fights.

Sigurd attributes his being more confident to having to constantly travel around the world to learn martial arts. He says, "After I started martial arts, I wanted to train more so I started to travel a lot more and in the process became more social. Because you will always get to meet new people on your travels." Last year, he travelled to Japan, Brazil, Italy, France, Sweden, and England to train in the various martial disciplines. Like some of the men, Sigurd is relatively wealthy to have the leisure to engage in these travels.

After his stay in at the gym, Sigurd has plans to head down south to Phuket to train at the gyms there. His travel plans for the rest of the year includes travelling to Vietnam and Cambodia. After Christmas, he plans to go back to Brazil to train again.

Stefan is a 22-year-old German undergraduate. This is his second visit to the gym. His first visit 2 years back was because he heard of David's reputation and the fact that he and his friend wanted to do something aside from what was the norm then, travelling to one of the islands in Spain to party. The positive experiences he had made him decide on making a trip back to the gym during his university break.

He has been learning Muay Thai for about 2 years and Brazilian Jiu Jitsu for about a year. He likes martial arts because they give him "a full workout. Helps me to get into shape and especially because I feel familiar at the gym and I have a lot of friends there." Physically stronger than before, Stefan candidly admits that his current physique is attractive to the ladies.

Stefan is currently back in Germany pursuing his degree course. He takes time off to train in Muay Thai whenever the opportunity presents itself.

Venkat is a 25-year-old professional fighter from India. His first trip to Kwaan-saa-maat Gym was in 2006. This trip to the gym is an opportunity for him to take a break from his other businesses and concentrate on honing his skills as a fighter, "to get the confidence back, to get the body back." Prior to coming to the gym, he was in Singapore competing in the One Fighting Championships and he was boasting how he got his first knockout within the first 20 seconds of the match. Venkat has been doing boxing and MMA for almost 11 years now. He switched from boxing to MMA because "MMA is a fast-growing combat sports," and he decided to compete in MMA because it provides him with the opportunity to "improve himself and prove that he is the best." This constant drive to improve himself is not operationalised as competing against other individuals but rather a competitive thing with himself. He views it as going out of his comfort zone and every time he will be performing better. I am going out of my comfort zone and every time I am performing better. Fighting for me is very honest because I am just fighting with myself. To make a certain decision, fighting with my entire relationship, fighting to compete." Venkat summarises this combat sport as "being a matter of reflections. That's how we try to play because as we prepare for our professional fights we will have our opponents' fight videos. So before a fight, we will strategise and train accordingly. Also when we fight, we try to figure out the loopholes of the other fighter and try to work out a strategy on the spot itself." Inevitably, in the course of his career, Venkat has sustained injuries in his ankle, shins, and shoulder blades.

With regards to his diet, Venkat comments that, as a fighter who travels around the world, he cannot afford to be choosy in what he eats. For him, supplements are an important part of his regime. In addition, because he is the spokesperson for a particular brand of supplements, he gets them for free. Using an analogy of a Honda and a Ferrari with the latter requiring premium fuel, Venkat argues that the body is similar in that if you want the body to function at its optimum, you need to feed it the best food available. He elaborates, "Supplements has to be a really important factor because by training you will wear and tear your muscles. And if you train every day or other alternate day, your body needs to recover. Otherwise because of the soreness, the pain in your body, your next timing suffers and you cannot perform better. So that's why you need to take supplements because we don't get enough macronutrients and those essential amino acids from the food itself. So when you take supplements, your body gets amino acids faster and it can perform better. So if you combine supplements with your diet, you have the feel good factor, you feel strong, you are ready for the next training regime where you can push your body again beyond the limit. Also your body wouldn't feel that much pain." However, he clarifies that for fighters there are always off seasons, seasons where there are fewer restrictions on their diet and lifestyle. It is only when there is an upcoming fight that he will strictly regulate his diet.

Reflexively, Venkat comments that his body has changed because of these regimes. His body now possesses faster reflexes and he says, "I feel faster, faster in the kicks, faster in blocking." In addition, he feels that the discipline instilled in him from practising martial arts is also transferable to other aspects of his life because the discipline "gives you the willpower to do different kind of things."

For Venkat, one of the pressing issues of being a professional fighter is the issue of money. He talks about the need to balance between training to be a professional fighter and managing and promoting himself for upcoming fights. He views the recent commercialisation of martial arts as being beneficial to him because "in the States and the Asian countries there are so many opportunities to go out and fight and get good money." However, the lifespan of a professional fighter is a short one because the life is hard not only physically but also in terms of the sacrifices such as "there [being] no personal life. You cannot spend time with your family and you are not financially independent." Despite knowing that his career as a professional fighter will not last, he argues, "You cannot stop doing martial arts. Martial arts can be practiced your whole life. You can train your whole life and keep yourself fit."

Venkat is training hard and travelling around the world, competing.

Vernon is a 28-year-old Indian who is also a Singaporean Permanent Resident. He is currently taking a year off work. Aside from training in Muay Thai in Thailand, he has plans to travel around the world, and see the sights. He is relatively new to Muay Thai having done it regularly for only 3 months. He is attracted to Muay Thai because it feels more "real than Taekwondo and Judo. Muay Thai is more real because it is a combat sport and it has more function for street fights when you have to defend yourself. It is aggressive and strong." Veron enjoys his stay at the gym because not only is "Muay Thai a very challenging and demanding exercise that is more of a mental exercise than anything else," but also at the gym, he gets "to mix up with other kinds of people who have the same interest. You meet up with amazing people, amazing fighters and understanding their reason for fighting and learning Muay Thai is also impressive. People come from all walks of life. There are electricians, there are street fighters, and there are university students who learn Muay Thai. So understanding what works for them inspires me." Unsurprisingly, he views sparring as a "mental game because you want to see if you can out-think the other guy in beating him. In sparring, it probably makes you a bit more thick-skinned to take pains and punches but more importantly it is just about outthinking the other guy and punching him back. So it is played as a mental game."

Vernon feels that Thailand is the best place to learn Muay Thai because "it is the origins of Muay Thai and Thailand is the place where the people are passionate about it." However, Vernon is a bit leery of Muay Thai gyms that are overly commercialised because "they have packages and they try to sell one on one personal packages. The trainers are still Thai but the driver for the training is not the passion to transfer skills but is more for the money. So yeah the trainers will still be motivated but it is not as personal anymore."

Muay Thai has taught him "focus and discipline." His body has been transformed by the regimes of Muay Thai and his leaner body now has greater stamina, strength. Vernon comments that he now watches his diet. He says, "Diet in general refers to just eating healthy, reducing junk food such as sugar. So it is less sugar, less carbs, a lot of protein." Being quite a jovial person, he jokes about how he has lost so much weight that he needs a change in his wardrobe. This translates to Muay Thai being a very expensive sport! The opportunity costs of leaving his job to learn Muay Thai is worth it because by allowing him to solely concentrate on Muay Thai, he is in "the best shape ever."

Despite his current passion for Muay Thai, Vernon knows that his interest in Muay Thai will be "seasonal because I take up Muay Thai too late in my life to pursue it professionally. After a while, it will die down but I think what I do take away from this experience is a passion for healthy living and having more confidence for self-defense. Even though I may not practice Muay Thai, I think I will practice a lot of things I learnt here. It may not be age but it might be of my work or other ventures that I am dealing in. I may not have enough time that Muay Thai needs. It is not a sport that you can do like once a week and feel happy about it. If you want to go into it you have to go into it a bit seriously more than that. On an average like three or four times a week basis. Because if you do it just once you will probably see a deterioration in the quality of the skills. It is like working out at the gym? You need to put in some time before you can see the results."

Summarising up his stay at the gym, Vernon says, "Looking at the last 3 months, I achieved quite a bit which I am happy with." After his stay at the gym, he is heading over to Chiang Mai to participate in a 10-day medication camp at a Buddhist monastery. He says the reason for this is because "it is like a different game. A mental game. Here [Kwaan-saa-maat Gym] I know that I can push myself but I also need to push my mental game to improve my physical game. Because in real life, you will have far too many injuries which will put you down so you need to be good mentally to keep going, to keep getting bigger and better." Vernon is still travelling the world and is currently in Brazil enjoying the good life.

Wan is a 33-year-old Canadian professional fighter. For the past 12 years, he has been competing professionally and teaching MMA in various parts of Asia, like Taiwan, Thailand, Singapore, and Hong Kong. Despite being a highly transnationally mobile individual, Wan professes that it is unlikely that he will ever go back to Canada to make a livelihood because most of his peers are already highly successful in their respective careers and he has to start again from the bottom of the hierarchy. He jokes that maybe he can start a Muay Thai school there in the future.

Wan is still competing professionally and his name is making waves within the Asian MMA circuit.

APPENDIX B: INTERVIEW SCHEDULE

1. How long have you been in Thailand?
   To find out more about the informant's biography.
2. What made you decide to come to Thailand to practise Muay Thai for a considerable duration? Are there opportunity costs to learning Muay Thai in Thailand?
   To find out more about why individuals come to Thailand to train, what sparked off their interest in Muay Thai, and why not just train

in their home countries. Issues of transnationalism and commercialisation may be pertinent here.

3. How long have you been practising Muay Thai? What made you decide to take up Muay Thai? Why not some other martial arts?
4. What to you is Muay Thai? What would you define as "good" Muay Thai?
5. What sustains your interest in practising or learning more about Muay Thai?
6. Have you invested a lot of time, money, and effort in Muay Thai? Do you think it is worth it?
7. Do you consider practising Muay Thai to be expensive activity in Thailand?
8. How do you think Muay Thai has impacted your life? For example, attitude or outlook?
9. Have you previously gotten into a fight or imagine yourself getting into a fight?
10. Compared to the past, do you think that by practising Muay Thai, the way in which your body functions in carrying out routine daily activities has changed? For example, do you think that there are improvements in your psychomotor skills?
11. Do you foresee a time when you will stop practising Muay Thai?

References

Green, D. C., & Chalip, L. (1988). Sport tourism as the celebration of subculture. *Annals of Tourism Research, 25*(1), 275–291.

Lefebvre, H. (1991b). *The production of social space* (2nd ed.) (D. Nicholson-Smith, Trans.). Malden, MA: Blackwell.

Leiter, J. (2005). Structural isomorphism in Australian nonprofit organisations. *International Journal of Voluntary and Nonprofit Organisation, 16*(1), 1–31.

Merleau-Ponty, M. (1965). *The structure of behaviour* (A. L. Fisher, Trans.). London: Methuen.

Roderick, M., Waddington, I., & Parker, G. (2000). Playing hurt: Managing injuries in English professional football. *International Review for the Sociology of Sport, 35*(2), 165–180.

Stewart, L. (1995). Bodies, visions and spatial politics: A review essay on Henri Lefebvre's the production of space. *Environment and Planning D: Society and Space, 13*(1), 609–618.

Stryker, S. (1987). Identity theory: Developments and extensions. In K. Yardley & T. Honess (Eds.), *Identity: Self and psychosocial perspectives*. New York: Wiley.

INDEX

W
Wacquant, L., 19, 76
 Body and Soul, Notebooks of an Apprentice Boxer, 19
Wai Khru Ram Muay, 76
Wan, 20, 21, 56, 83, 128

Williams, D., 25
World Wai Kru Muay Thai Ceremony, 2015, 2
Writing Culture (Clifford and Marcus), 29

The manufacturer's authorised representative in the EU is Springer
Nature Customer Service Centre GmbH, Europaplatz 3, 69115 Heidelberg,
Germany. If you have any concerns regarding our products, please
contact ProductSafety@springernature.com

Printed and bound by CPI Group (UK) Ltd, Croydon, CR0 4YY
23/04/2026
02095601-0010